090

EUROPEAN IMPRESSIONS OF THE NEW ENGLAND COAST 1497–1620

Douglas R. Mc Manis

Teachers College,
Columbia University

THE UNIVERSITY OF CHICAGO
DEPARTMENT OF GEOGRAPHY
RESEARCH PAPER NO. 139

1972

Library of Congress Catalog Card Number: 70-187026

Research Papers are available from:
The University of Chicago
Department of Geography
5828 S. University Avenue
Chicago, Illinois 60637
Price: $5.00 list; $4.00 series subscription

ACKNOWLEDGEMENTS

During the decade or more in which the author has been collecting materials on the historical geography of New England he has accumulated debts of gratitude to many librarians, archivists, and local historians who have shared their collections and knowledge. Appreciation for their services is extended to all of them with the hope that they find the monograph worthy of their contributions. The staff of the Map Division of the Library of Congress deserves a special notice for making a long research period there pleasant and productive in spite of Washington's summer heat. With a nostalgia that comes with increasing years away from graduate school, Professors Marvin W. Mikesell of the University of Chicago and Wesley C. Calef now of Illinois State University are remembered for encouraging me to select areal assessment and imagery as a field of long term study. Colleagues and the secretarial staff of the Department of Social Studies, Teachers College, Columbia University as well as the College administration have aided me in ways too numerous to list. Finally a special thanks to Professors Moya and James Andrews who supplied the interest and encouragement that only friends can provide during the toil of writing.

Douglas R. Mc Manis
Teachers College
Columbia University
New York, New York

May 28, 1971

TABLE OF CONTENTS

LIST OF ILLUSTRATIONS

INTRODUCTION

In the years following the Columbian discovery of the New World the Atlantic seaboard of North America was the scene of many sporadic visits by seafaring Europeans, but for over a century it remained on the periphery of European New World activities which were concentrated in the West Indies, Mexico, or parts of South America. Yet those irregular visits were the initial contacts between the seaboard and Western Europeans which laid the foundations for its later transformation into a landscape dominated by European cultural patterns and processes. For this monograph one seaboard zone which was the locale of such initial Europeanization has been selected for study--the New England coast from Passamaquoddy Bay, Maine, to Cape Cod. The period of study begins in 1497 or 1498 with the first known European visit after Columbus' first voyage and extends to 1620--the year in which permanent European settlement of the coast commenced at Plymouth, Massachusetts.

The settlement at Plymouth was not an isolated event but rather was part of a continuum of European contacts with the coast which had been occurring during the century and a quarter which is the period of this study. This period which preceded the spread of English population throughout the coast and its hinterland was significant because it was the prelude in which the principal themes to be developed later were introduced. During that period Europeans engaged in two basic types of processes not only for the New England coast but other areas of the New World as well--collection of data about the area and the translation of the reports of strange places and people into descriptions which were meaningful to Europeans.

The period began with the region's existence barely proved. Its extent, configuration, relationship to adjacent lands, and physical and cultural geography were total unknowns. At the end of the period accurate data on those topics were available, although they

1

were not always recognized as such and misconceptions persisted.
The collection of regional data and their availability in Europe did
not accrue in a steady progression throughout the period. In the
earliest years fragmentary sketches were based on reports from
voyages which touched briefly only a few locales along the littoral.
While the middle years yielded some new data, unfortunately they
were scanty and included fanciful and inaccurate items. Not until
the last two decades of the period was there anything which could
be described as systematic and accurate surveys of the coast made
and reported to Europe. The relative neglect in which the coast
had languished ended at the start of the seventeenth century when
English and French explorers visited the coast with some frequency.
Although the reports from those expeditions continued to perpetuate
some misconceptions and fanciful ideas about the region and were
sometimes distorted by the prose of promoters, in general they
maintained a high level of objectivity and accurate description.
Needless to say, those two decades were most critical in determining the future character of the area.

Ideally new information about the region should have given
added depth to European understanding of the area's geography or
should have corrected lingering misconceptions. In some cases
that happened, but in others it did not. Particularly during the
sixteenth century portion of the study period Europeans were apt
to blend the scanty available data to preconceptions such as the
parallel distribution of phenomena throughout the world or the
existence of a passage to the Pacific Ocean, to accept as fact meager hints of the presence of precious metals and gems, and to perpetuate stereotyped cartographic depictions of the area. From
such data and their haphazard manner of collection, Europeans
attempted to make meaningful representations and images of the
area.

Instead of a single view of the region's geography, several
representations were formulated. While each contained some
basis of fact, all had elements of fancy, dreams of precious wealth,
and incompleteness. Not until the last two decades of the period
were systematic reports by competent observers available to shift
fact from fancy. But even before then--in the last quarter of the
sixteenth century the English and French had enough experience

with the coast to know that fish and furs were exploitable wealth there. The English used that evidence as well as their desire to control the elusive Northwest Passage and the need for a station to sustain their encroachments in the Spanish West Indies to develop a scheme for an English outpost somewhere along the coast. The scheme came to naught, but the ideas of the coast as part of an English overseas empire and of a resident European population there were henceforth to be part of the speculation about the coast's future. While such ideas from the hindsight of history pointed the direction of later developments, in the study period their validity was not immediately apparent, and they shared currency with other ideas which resisted change or abandonment.

In this monograph five essays examine the changing impressions held by Europeans of the New England coast during the first century and a quarter in which it was known to them. In order to get the reader as close as possible to the events, people, and their ideas about the coast, contemporary records of explorers, maps, official materials, and promotional literature are the principal sources for the text. In some instances passages are cited at length because they retain the flavor of the period which would be lost by paraphrase and hopefully will convey directly to the reader something of the wonder and excitement which surrounded those happenings.

The first essay deals with the various cartographic styles which were devised for the coast. Because maps comprise the largest body of extant primary sources from the early part of the period, the major European impressions of that era are discussed in relation to the cartographic depictions. Iberian and Italian impressions of the area, which became relatively unimportant in the later years of the period, except as perpetuated stereotyped cartographic styles, were the basis of dominant styles throughout the sixteenth century and thus have a prominent position in this essay. Because of the inaccurate character of area's portrayal on these early maps, attention is given to the interpretative controversies which surround them. The achievement of realistic cartographic representation of the coast was made by the English and French in the last two decades of the study period, and the essay concludes with that achievement.

The remainder of the monograph focuses primarily on English impressions and secondarily on French ones. One essay has French survey of the coast and their evaluation and rejection of it as a site for a permanent fur trade as principal themes. This essay also identifies the importance of economic sub-groups in national decisions about the area, for, although the activities are labelled French, only a small group of Frenchmen involved in the fur trade participated in the survey and the resultant decision that the coast was unsatisfactory for their purpose. Other potential which they associated with it was ignored. The text of this essay is based on the writings and maps of Samuel de Champlain who not only was a member of the expeditions which surveyed the entire length of the coast without, however, entering all of its numerous indentations but also was an incomparable evaluator of what he saw. A brief excursion into the area to found a Jesuit mission to the Maine Indians was thwarted by Virginians and illustrates the competition which was emerging between England and France for actual control of North American areas and was to continue until the last half of the eighteenth century. That episode is based chiefly on the account of the Jesuit father who led the mission.

England's relationship to the area is in many ways perplexing to understand, especially in the sixteenth century when its short spans of active interest were separated by long intervals of dis-interest. Three essays focus on the changing English impressions of the coast. A late Elizabethan scheme which projected the even-tual transplanting of a model of English society across the Atlantic is the subject of one essay. In their efforts to evaluate the worth of the scheme potential backers collected available information about the region, known to them as Norembega. In doing so they compiled the sources which are detailed in the essay for its first regional geography. However, the data illustrated more the con-temporary limitations of knowledge than its accuracy or compre-hensiveness. In the early seventeenth century as English ambiguity toward the coast ended explorers, fishermen, and fur traders came there. From their enthusiastic reports and evidence of exploitable wealth which they provided promoters were able to portray the area as one worthy of English control, and powerful men interested in overseas expansion centered their activities there. But the idea that the region was habitable received a sharp setback when a colonial failure was associated with a harsh climate. These themes are the content of the second essay on English impressions. The final essay is concerned with the beginnings of permanent European settlement on the coast. The idea of such settlement was old by the time it became an actuality. The reason for settlement at some place along the coast and the process of selecting a satisfactory site are the main topics of this essay. Proof that Englishmen could make their homes there was demonstrated by a small band of exiles. While this monograph ends on that theme, the event itself marks the start of processes which eventually transformed the coast and its hinterland into a <u>new</u> England.

CHAPTER I

CARTOGRAPHIC STYLES OF THE
NEW ENGLAND COAST

Cartographic styles of the New England coast are only one segment of the larger history of New World cartography. In contrast to the other types of documentary evidence for the period of this study surviving maps provide a continuous record of the changing European knowledge and conceptions of the North American continent's geography. For much of the first century after Columbus' discovery of the New World, European interest centered on the West Indies, a fabled northwest passage, and locales of possible treasure hordes. Those concerns resulted in map representations of the Caribbean area, Newfoundland, and South America much earlier than for any part of the United States. The cartographic history and styles of the New England coast began with the explorations of the northwest Atlantic undertaken by various non-Spanish countries, although Spain itself was briefly active in the region--long enough to make a dominant contribution to the coast's images on the Ribero type maps (Figure 1). [1]

Newfoundland and nearby areas are the first parts of northeastern North America to appear on European maps. Those regions were drawn in two styles. Cartographers who accepted the theory that Asia was the land mass involved afixed the sailors' discoveries as the northeastern portions of that continent as did Contarini in 1506 [2] or as a group of embayed peninsulas attached to that

---

[1] Since this manuscript was completed, Samuel E. Morison's comprehensive study of early European exploration has appeared but too late for his ideas to be used here. His work touches upon many topics discussed in this chapter and elsewhere in the monograph and should be consulted by anyone interested in the subject. See Morison, Samuel E., The European Discovery of America: The Northern Voyages (New York: Oxford University Press, 1971).

[2] Skelton, R. A., Explorers' Maps (New York: Frederick A. Praeger, 1958),

6

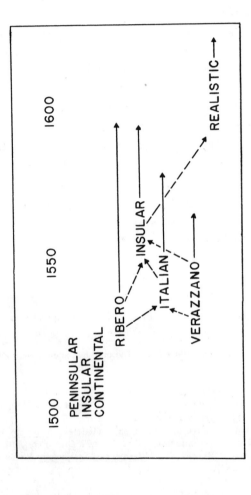

Fig. 1.--Cartographic Styles of the New England Coast: Chronology and Interrelations

continent as did Ruysch on his map for the 1507 and 1508 Rome editions of Ptolemy's atlas.[3]

Closer to reality, however, was the insular style wherein the
northwest Atlantic lands were portrayed as one or more islands
hanging isolated in the ocean (Figure 2). The main characteristic
of this style was a crescent-shaped island with numerous bays and
peninsulas on its eastern side while the western flank was an undif-
ferentiated line.[4] Portuguese sources were paramount here, for
the figures were usually identified as "Terra del Rey de Portugal"
or "Terra Cortereal." Also they were displaced eastward in longitude so that they appeared to be on the Portuguese side of the
dividing meridian established by the Treaty of Tordesillas. As
more information on these high mid-latitude areas was acquired
and the Portuguese ceased their activity in the northwest Atlantic,
the crescent-shaped style and its nomenclature were abandoned.[5]

A significantly different image contemporaneous with the peninsular and insular styles is found on the map of Juan de la Cosa.
This map depicts the coast of North America as a single line--
hence showing a large land mass from high to low latitudes where
a portrait of St. Christopher covers the isthmus of Panama, a
device which left ambiguous the continuity of the Americas. The

---

fig. 36 and p. 72 for reproduction and discussion of this map. The original is in the British Museum.

[3]Library of Congress copy used for this study. The map has such a peninsula called "Terra Nova."

[4]Examples of this style are the Cantino map of 1502, the Kunstmann I and II, and the King-Hamy map. The Cantino map is reproduced in Cortesão, Armando, and da Mota, Avelino T., Portugaliae Monumenta Cartographica (Lisbon: n.p., 1960), Vol. I, pp. 7-13, plates 4-5. The Kunstmann maps are in Kunstmann, Friedrich, Atlas zur Entdeck-ungsgeschichte Amerikas (Munich: in commission bei A. Asher & Cie, 1859), Blatt I-II. The King-Hamy map is reproduced in Bagrow, L., History of Cartography (London: C. A. Watts & Co., 1964), plate LVIII.

[5]These crescent-shaped islands suggest a stylistic relationship to Vinland as drawn on the Vinland map. There it is depicted in a comparable outline, although it is not as obviously half-moon, lacks numerous indentations, and is cruder in execution. But the resemblance is striking enough to postulate the stylistic relationship. If the Vinland map is a stylistic prototype of these later maps, it would date the map closer to the early six-teenth century than some of its proponents currently admit. The postulation would also involve how the style was transferred to the drawer of the Vinland map. See Skelton, R. A., et al., Vinland Map and Tartar Relation (New Haven: Yale University Press, 1964), pp. 105ff.

Fig. 2.--The Insular Style: A Portion of Kunstmann II (courtesy of the American History Division, The New York Public Library, Astor, Lenox and Tilden Foundations).

lack of distinctive coastal features such as Florida, the Gulf of
Mexico, or large embayments suggests that the compiler or the
cartographer for much of the map's western half was "filling in the
map," a technique which was absent from later Spanish New World
cartography where unknown areas were frequently left blank.[6] Nevertheless, this map is unique because it is the oldest surviving
map to convey the contiguousness of northern new lands without
direct identification of them as the east coast of Asia, but there is
on it no indication whether the maker conceived of them as extensions of Asia or as an independent continent.[7]

The map is a controversial and confusing document. Its
author is assumed to be Juan de la Cosa, pilot on Columbus' first
and second voyages. Although there is on it the date 1500, several
scholars have advanced arguments not only that it was made later,
perhaps about 1508, but also that the surviving copy is not the original and that Cosa's conceptions were probably victims of copyists'
alterations.[8]

The map's mid-latitude section is the only North American
portion considered here. The northern end of this section was
identified as being discovered by the English. Small flags with
the arms of England dot this part of the coast, and a short legend
identifies it as belonging to the king of England. The "English
Coast" raises two unresolved questions: (1) what was the author's
authority for an English discovery and its relationship to the date

[6]Taylor, E. G. R., Tudor Geography 1485-1583 (New York: Octagon Books, 1968), p. 11; Wroth, L. C., The Voyages of Giovanni da Verrazzano 1525-1528 (New Haven: Yale University Press, 1970), p. 169.

[7]Skelton, Explorers' Maps, p. 71, thinks that the compiler conceived of them as an extension of Asia. If true, then the map differed from the Contarini-Ruysch style in degree, not kind.

[8]Crone, G. R., Maps and Their Makers (London: Hutchinson & Co., 1968), pp. 79-81; Ganong, W. F., Crucial Maps in the Early Cartography and Place-Nomenclature of the Atlantic Coast of Canada (Toronto: University of Toronto Press, 1964), pp. 140-72; Nunn, G. E., The la Cosa Map and the Cabot Voyages (Jenkintown: Tall Tree Library, 1946), and The Mappemonde of Juan de la Cosa (Jenkintown: George H. Bean Library, 1934); Parry, J. H., The Age of Reconnaissance (London: Weidenfeld and Nicolson, 1963), p. 104; Roukema, E., "Some Remarks on the La Cosa Map," Imago Mundi, XIV (1959), 38-54; Williamson, J. A. (ed.), The Cabot Voyages and Bristol Discovery under Henry VII (Cambridge: Hakluyt Society, 1962), pp. 72-83. The map hangs in the Museo Naval, Madrid, Spain.

of the map, and (2) what is the real equivalent of Cosa's "English Coast (Figure 3)?"

Other than sailings from Bristol in the 1470's and 80's into the north Atlantic in search of the mythical island of Brazil, the earliest English ventures into the unknown waters to the west were the voyages of the Cabots under the sponsorship of Henry VII to find a northwest passage to Cathay. Information about the Cabots probably was the basis of Cosa's "English Coast." Official records state that John Cabot and his three sons were twice, 1497 and 1498, commissioned by King Henry VII, but also there are hints of an earlier voyage sponsored by Bristol merchants and a later one by Sebastian Cabot alone in the first decade of the sixteenth century.[9] The records, however, are not clear as to which Cabot led the two royal expeditions, where they explored, or indeed if they actually sailed. Authorities of the early sixteenth century, mostly Spanish and Portuguese, consistently agreed in ascribing the leadership to Sebastian Cabot, that the land of the Baccallaos (land of the cod-fish) was discovered by him, and that after venturing north of the Baccallaos, he sailed south to about 34° north latitude from whence he returned to England.[10] Based on these sources, Hoffman concluded that the Cosa map memorialized a 1508 (circa) voyage by Sebastian.[11] In terms of the available evidence and the state of the Cosa map, such a conclusion seems somewhat arbitrary, especially on the matter of the discovery of the Baccallaos so late. That region had appeared on maps in the insular and peninsular styles before 1508 as a result of the Cortereal voyages. If we accept Hoffman's date, we must accept the premise that Sebastian

---

[9] See Williamson, op. cit., for the known documents on the Cabots. Interpretative materials include Quinn, D. B., "The Argument for the English Discovery of America between 1480 and 1494," Geographical Journal, CXXVII (1961), 277-85, and Vigneras, L. A., "New Light on the 1497 Cabot Voyage to America," Hispanic American Historical Review, XXXVI (1956), 503-9.

[10] Peter Martyr, Oviedo, and Gomara were writing when Sebastian Cabot was Pilot Major of Spain and giving himself sole credit for the voyages, although he wrote no personal memoir of the voyages. See Hoffman, B. G., Cabot to Cartier (Toronto: University of Toronto Press, 1961), pp. 16-25. For rejection of Hoffman's conclusions on Cabot and the Cosa map, see Wroth, op. cit., p. 39.

[11] Hoffman, op. cit., p. 97. For differing opinions see Oleson, T. J., Early Voyages and Northern Approaches 1000-1632 (Toronto: McClellan and Stewart, 1963), pp. 128, 136-37.

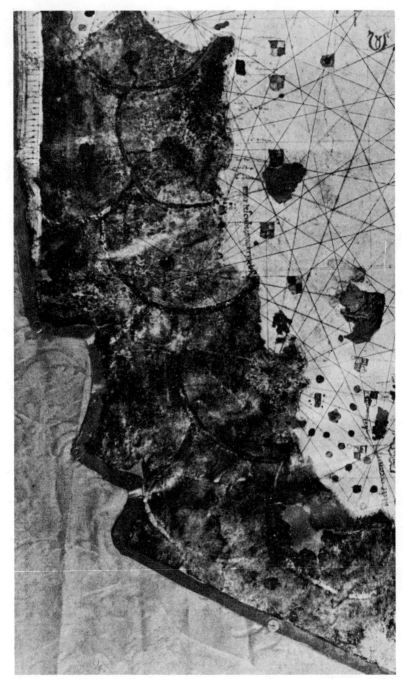

Fig. 3. -- The Continental Style: The Northeastern New World Section of the Cosa Map

Cabot did not reveal the land of the codfish to Europe. If the claim that a Cabot discovered the region is valid, it must have been done before the Cortereals--or before 1501. Therefore if Cosa had Cabot data, it was from the 1497-98 voyages of which we have some official evidence. Further implication for the earlier date of the map's construction is the fact that the authorities on whom Hoffman premised a 1508 voyage knew of the Cortereal expeditions, a circumstance which leaves the question of why they should attribute the discovery of one region simultaneously to several individuals. [12]

Hoffman's thesis for the Cabot material not only requires acceptance of the later construction date for the Cosa map but also implies that the 1508 dating may be too early because some interval was needed between Cabot's supposed return and the drawing of the map. Still, the large western land masses could be later copyist additions, made in an effort to keep the map contemporary. His hypothesized coincidence, based on photographic distortion of scale and orientation, between a section of Cosa's map and the Refugio-Luisa part of Verazzano's planisphere, if true, suggests additions after 1524. [13] But if the motive was to keep the map up-to-date, then why were not Florida, the Gulf of Mexico, or the isthmus of Panama added for the same purpose? Since they were not placed on it, the answer is probably that the present state of the map is close to the original version and that copyist additions were minimal. With this interpretation the Refugio-Luisa coincidence becomes validation that Cabot preceded Verazzano to the area.

A circa 1508 date for the Cosa map, however, makes the land mass depiction more explicable than an earlier date, but perhaps the compiler was a more astute interpreter of New World data than Columbus himself. Cabot data from the 1497-98 voyages augmented by information from fishermen already using the northwest Atlantic fisheries could have supported the existence of a continent without

---

[12] The thesis that Cortereals' Lavrador was Greenland is here pertinent because those early authorities might have associated them with Greenland (Labrador) and Cabot with Newfoundland. See Morison, S. E., _Portuguese Voyages to America in the Fifteenth Century_ (Cambridge: Harvard University Press, 1940), for discussion of the voyages of the Cortereals and their probable dates.

[13] Hoffman, _op. cit._, p. 96.

supplying details about its configuration. In 1508 a compiler could have data on which to project a northern continent; in 1500 such a land mass would have been a "wild guess" or a matter of belief. These are undocumented suppositions. Until additional evidence is available, it is concluded that the Cosa map is the oldest surviving cartographic representation of the Cabot discoveries made in 1497 or 1498. Because of its imprecise coastal configuration, the Cosa map illustrates as do the other two map images the vague status of European knowledge of the area under study.

The configuration of the mid-latitude North American coast on the Cosa map resembles a series of inverted steps.[14] That coast line is a series of east-west lines of varying length connected together by lines on a nearly north-south axis to give the area a gradual westward descent in latitude.[15] The "English Coast" occurs on one of the longest east-west sections. Regardless of scale, there is no part of the North American Atlantic coast with a comparable east-west dimension except along the Gulf of Mexico. Although that orientation is explained as an error of magnetic declination, the early chronicles were quite specific about a southward, not westward, course. It remains to be explained why the cartographer did not adjust his coast to the stated course, if one accepts that the ship paralleled the coast. But it is possible that the chroniclers referred only to the general course, while the map retained deviations made in following the coast line. But whatever the probable explanations of discrepancies, the map's coastal configuration has no apparent counterpart on the modern map.

---

[14]The map does not have parallels or meridians, but the European part of it is probably as accurate in its relative locations as any map of the period. Latitude, longitude, or linear distance is impossible to determine on the New World portion of the map. It is obviously on a scale different from that of the Old World portion. The only indisputable New World features are the West Indies, where Cuba and Hispaniola are both completely north of the Tropic of Cancer, a typical placement for them on maps of that era. With such total distortion approximations of latitudes, longitudes, or distances would be meaningless.

[15]A long expanse of east-west coast for this part of North America is found on many maps of the middle and late sixteenth century. The origin of that tradition may be in errors of magnetic declination as the coast was explored by Europeans. But such alignments when the records stated courses of other orientations and the use of the east-west lines for areas still unknown to Europeans suggest that the east-west orientation of the coastline had become a stylistic stereotype. See Skelton, Explorers' Maps, figs. 36, 39, and 44 for other examples.

As has been mentioned only the "English Coast" correlates with recorded visits to the continent, and it may be assumed that elsewhere the coast is based chiefly on the cartographer's conjectures. Even if one accepts the premise of a Cabot sailing as far south as 34° north, the data available to the compiler were meager. Here in sum are the surviving details of the Cabots. The voyagers after crossing the North Atlantic sighted land which they called the land of codfish. Sailing northward until stopped by ice masses, they reversed course and cruised southward to approximately 34° north. On the southern journey there is no mention of landings or how close they might have gone to shore. No description by anyone on the voyages has been found. The lack of coastal differentiation on the map indicates that its compiler had no more data than are currently available. [16]

It is assumed that the easternmost end of the "English Coast" was or was near the Cabot landfall, a point which is usually placed somewhere on Newfoundland or Cape Breton Island. [17] Even with such an established point there is in these latitudes no long east-west coast which may be proposed as the equivalent of the map's line, unless one uses a distorted Nova Scotian littoral as the answer to the puzzle. One recent attempt to resolve the dilemma utilized the place name nomenclature to identify the types of places described on the map. The sequence of land and water bodies identified when plotted at a reduced scale on a modern map gave a reasonable approximation of a traverse from southeastern Newfoundland to Miramichi Bay, New Brunswick. [18] In this interpretation the map's coastline becomes a route, not a pattern of coastal configuration. But to accept the theory that Cosa's "English Coast" is a route is inconsistent with the cartographic techniques elsewhere on

[16] The question of why Sebastian Cabot during his Spanish career or later never composed his version of the voyages is intriguing but beyond the scope of this work. He needs a biographer.

[17] See Ganong, op. cit., pp. 12, 201, 232, for the case for a Cape Breton landfall; arguments for a Newfoundland landfall appear in the works of G. R. F. Prowse whose bibliography is found in Ganong, op. cit., p. 478. Parry, op. cit., p. 154, accepts both possibilities.

[18] Davies, Arthur, "The 'English' Coast on the Map of Juan de la Cosa," Imago Mundi, XII (1956), 27.

the map. It is also impossible to link the New Brunswick terminus
with the remaining Atlantic portion of Cosa's coastline where there
are reasons to argue that the compiler used other Cabot data,
although the area was not designated as English and would be New
England. Studied in isolation the interpretation has merit, but in
the context of the total northeastern coast, it is unacceptable.

In the middle of the map's North American coast south and
west of the "English Coast" is a "step" which superficially may be
construed to be the New England coast, although at a grossly distorted scale. A crescent-shaped concave gulf ends on its southern
flank with an eastward projection west of which are a small bay
and a large one with an offshore island between them. These features may be respectively the Gulf of Maine, Cape Cod, Narragansett and Buzzards bays, and any one of the several islands along
the southern New England coast. [19] A river draining southeastward
enters the northern part of the gulf. It perhaps is an early portrayal of the Rio de las Gamas which appeared on later Spanish
maps and is usually assumed to be Penobscot Bay. West of the
smaller of the two adjacent bays the coast runs south by west and
has no distinguishing features. Because of the differences of features north and south of this point, it may mark the southern limit
of the compiler's Cabot data and hence the southern limit of Cabot's
cruise. If this be correct, Cabot may have gone no farther west
and south than Long Island instead of the 34° north of the early
chronicles. Unfortunately there exists no evidence by which these
conjectures may be corroborated, and we leave the Cosa map with
the conclusion that it raises more problems than it resolves. As
an example of an image of the New England coast, it symbolizes
the coast's then unknown status in Europe.

No significant image of the New England coast is found in New
World cartography of the sixteenth century's second decade. The
portrayal of the area, in fact, appears regressive from the earlier
images. During this decade official interest in the area was limited; fishermen possibly frequented the waters of the Northwest

---

[19] This is the section where Hoffman found the coincidence with Verazzano's Refugio-
Luisa. See Hoffman, op. cit., p. 96.

Atlantic, and there is evidence of other commercial activities.[20]
But in spite of these possible sources of new information, the few
surviving maps of the decade portray nothing new or have little on
them to indicate that new data were returned from those brief contacts. An example of this cartography is the Lopo Homem map of
1519.[21] The contrast between North and South America on this map
is striking. South America, called Terra Novus Brazil, had its
northeast quadrant in a recognizable shape. The West Indies were
depicted with an accuracy customary for the period, although Cuba
was truncated on its western end in such a fashion that it could be
either an island or a peninsula. In contrast where known parts of
North America (i. e. Baccallaos, Florida, or the Gulf of Mexico)
should be were only fragmented pieces of land along the map's western margin. There is no indication either by configuration or by
label whether the cartographer conceived these bits of land as
extensions of Asia, as separate islands, or as synonymous with
areas reported in earlier explorations.

Ribero and Verazzano Styles

During the third decade of the sixteenth century the situation
was radically changed when the voyages of Gomez and Verazzano
supplied data for mapmakers to depict the mid-latitude areas of
the North American coast. Coastal configurations and nomencla-
tures which originated in these two voyages were to dominate the
cartographic images of the New England coast for the remainder of
the century.

Esteban Gomez sailed from Coruña either late in 1524 or
early in 1525 to search for the northwest passage to Cathay along
the uncharted coast south of the Baccallaos and north of Florida.[22]

---

[20]Reed, Arthur, "John Rastell's Voyage in the Year 1517, " Mariner's Mirror, IX
(May, 1923), 137-47.

[21]Heawood, Edward, "Lopo Homem's Map of 1519, " Geographical Journal, LXXVII
(March, 1931), 250-55.

[22]Gomez had been a pilot on the Magellan expedition but abandoned the fleet along the
coast of South America. Although Magellan's cruise proved the existence of a route
around the New World to the Pacific Ocean, because of hazardous sailing conditions of the
southern straits, the Spanish never conceived of the passage as a feasible commercial

After Ayllon's exploration of the southern coast in 1521-22, the Spanish had some knowledge of the entire eastern coast of North America from Florida north to Cape Race except for the mid-latitude portion where Gomez was directed to investigate. The official reports of the expedition are lost. Maps constructed from its data remain the principal source of information about the voyage, for most contemporary Spanish narratives or chronicles contain only brief passages which stressed the ridicule heaped on Gomez for his return with only a cargo of slaves.[23]

The longest and most detailed description of Gomez' voyage is found in Islario General del Mundo by the Pilot-Major Santa Cruz and written several decades after the voyage. Because of his official position Santa Cruz probably had access to the now lost documents. He wrote:

> Stephen Gomez, the pilot whom we have already mentioned in connection with the voyage and expedition which he made by the order and leave of Your Majesty, in search of and to discover Cathay, which is a city of East India, as well as the passage or strait so much desired, and leading to the sea commonly called the South Sea. It took him ten months, and he discovered on that coast a great many islands near the continent; and particularly a very large and deep river, which he called Deer River, on account of the great number of those animals which he found there. It is full of islands in which the Indians of the continent come to live in the summer, owing to large fisheries of salmon, shads, and pickerel as well as other species of fish which are found in that part of the stream. He sailed up the river for a considerable distance, thinking that it was the strait which he desired to discover, but ascertained instead that it was a grand river with a very great flow of water, from which he inferred that it belonged to the continent of immense size which is there. And although firmly believing in the existence of the aforesaid canal or passage close to the cod-fish continent and the country called Labrador, he was also convinced of the inutility of proving it experimentally, as the obstacles arising from the cold temperature of the neighbouring

---

route. Continued Spanish interest in finding a direct, usable route to the Pacific was manifested in Charles V's sponsorship of the Gomez voyage. See Harrisse, Henry, The Discovery of North America (Amsterdam: N. Israel, 1961 [reprint of 1892 London edition]), pp. 229-43, for discussion of the voyage and surviving sources of data. For a recent interpretation of the Gomez voyage based on fresh evidence consult Vigneras, L. A., "The Voyage of Esteban Gomez from Florida to the Baccalaos," Terrae Incognitae, II (1970), 25-28.

[23] Among the contemporary authorities who mentioned the Gomez voyage were Peter Martyr d'Anghiera, De Orbe Novo (1516); Oviedo y Valdes, Gonzalo, La Historia General de las Indias (1526); Galvano, Antonio, The Discoveries of the World (London: Hakluyt Society, 1857 [reprint of 1563 original]), pp. 167-68; Gomara, Francisco Lopez de, Historia General de las Indias (Madrid: Calpe, 1922 [reprint of 1552 original]), Vol. I, pp. 86-87. For the unhappy ending of the voyage as described by Martyr see MacNutt, F. A. (ed.), De Orbe Novo: The Eight Decades of Peter Martyr d'Anghiera (New York: G. P. Putnam's Sons, 1912), Vol. II, p. 418.

regions would prevent in the future any further attempt to effect the object. . . . [24]

Returning to the islands in Deer River and those lying off the neighbouring continent, these as I have already explained, are nearly all of them inhabited, principally in the summer by Indians like those of St. Domingo . . . , although these men and women have finer bodies. They sharpen the bows, arrows and spears with which they fight by toasting them. Their land has a temperate climate and is covered with the trees common to those regions such as evergreens, oaks and olives. Many wild vines are found which bear grapes, and many plants and herbs similar to Spain. There is much marcasite which they mistook for gold. They brought home to Spain in the galleon many Indians, whom they afterwards set at liberty. [25]

The earliest known appearance on maps of data from the Gomez expedition is found on the Castiglioni map of 1525. Much of this map was evidently drawn before Gomez sailed, and the results of his voyage added in a lighter line than the rest of the coast after his return. [26] The configuration of the coast comparable to that depicted on the Castiglioni map appeared on later maps drawn or designed by Diego Ribero, the Portuguese born royal cartographer of Spain. The "Weimar-Spanish" map of 1527 showed the northeastern coast so similar to authenticated Ribero maps that it was probably one of his. Two signed Ribero planispheres date from 1529 and are identified as the "Weimar Ribero" and the "Rome Ribero." [27] Another unsigned map know as the "Wolfenbüttel Spanish" (circa 1527-30) is also comparable enough to the signed maps to be classified as a Ribero. [28] The New England coastal configura-

---

[24] The translation of the first paragraph is cited from Harrisse, op. cit., pp. 243-35, where the Spanish text is also printed.

[25] This paragraph is quoted from Biggar, H. P. (ed.), The Precursors of Jacques Cartier 1497-1534, Vol. V. of Publications of the Canadian Archives (Ottawa: Government Printing Bureau, 1911), p. 194. It may also be found in Hoffman, op. cit., p. 116.

[26] Cortesão, Armando, "Note on the Castiglioni Planisphere," Imago Mundi, XI (1954), 53-55. The legend on this map in the latitude of Maine reads, "Land which was discovered by Estaban Gomez this year of 1525 by order of his Majesty." For a brief biography of Ribero, consult Vigneras, L. A., "The Cartographer Diogo Ribeiro," Imago Mundi, XVI (1962), 76-83.

[27] The title names refer to the archives where the maps are located. The Rome copy is in the Vatican Library, while others are in the former grand ducal library at Weimar. The Castiglioni map is in the Archivo Marchese Castiglione, Mantua, Italy. See Skelton, Explorers' Maps, Fig. 122 and p. 202, for a reproduction and discussion of the Rome copy, and Parry, op. cit., p. 105. Reproductions of these and other maps are in Nordenskiold, N. A. E., Facsimile Atlas (Stockholm: P. A. Norstedt & söner, 1889), and Perpiplus: An Essay on the Early History of Charts and Sailing Directions (Stockholm: P. A. Norstedt & söner, 1897).

[28] Stevenson, E. L., "Early Spanish Cartography of the New World," Proceedings of the American Antiquarian Society, New Series, XIX (1908-1909), 380.

tions and nomenclature on these five maps form an image appropriately called here the Ribero Style (Figure 4).

The Ribero image of the New England coast was marked by two prominent features: (1) a peninsula or cape projecting northeast from a latitude slightly below 40° north, and (2) a deep embayment stretching northward into the continent located northeast of the cape. Between these two features was a concave coast line broken by several small rivers. On the western side of the mouth of the large bay was a small peninsula and an offshore group of islands. East of the bay the coast ran nearly due east-west to Cape Breton and had numerous small indentions.

On the two signed Ribero maps the entire area was called Tiera de Estavã Gomez. On the Weimar copy the legend continued, ". . . which he discovered by order of His Majesty in the year 1525. It contains numerous trees and fruits like those of Spain and much rodovallo, salmon, and soles. No gold has been found." The same name was used on the unsigned Wolfenbüttel map, but its legend read, ". . . which he discovered in the year 1525 by command of His Majesty. It is well suited to yield breadstuff and wine in great abundance." The comparison of flora with those of Spain was as misleading as the Santa Cruz statement that olives grew there. Wine was another evidence that Gomez might have reported items to enhance the appeal of the area when he failed in the basic purpose of his mission, but delusions about the area's potentiality for wine production continued into the seventeenth century.

The name of the large cape appeared only on the "Weimar Ribero" and the "Wolfenbüttel-Spanish" as C. de Arenas; it was unidentified on the other three Riberos. On the former two the large bay was called Arecifas (Weimar copy) and Arenles (Wolfenbüttel copy). Like the peninsula it was unnamed on the other three. The cape west of the entrance of the bay was labelled C. de muchas ylas or islas on all except the Castiglioni version where it was unidentified. The island group was called the Arcipelago de Estavan Gomez on the two signed Riberos.

Taken as a complete unit, the Ribero coast from the bay south to the cape was a reasonable resemblance to the outline of the New England coast from Penobscot Bay to Cape Cod. These modern associations are the conclusions of many scholars, but dissenting

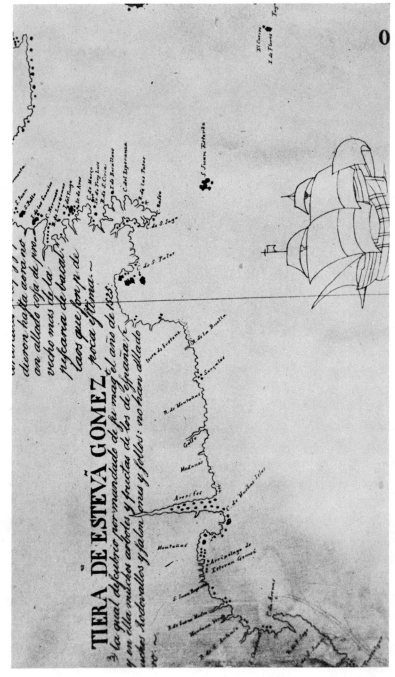

Fig. 4.--The Ribero Style: A Portion of a Ribero Planisphere (courtesy of the Library of Congress)

opinions have been defended with the data from the maps themselves. For those who accept the accuracy of the latitudes on the
Ribero maps the peninsula has been identified as Sandy Hook, Long
Island's eastern tip, or Cape Henelopen among others. In view of
the frequent inaccuracies of latitude on most early New World maps,
most investigators assume that the peninsula's latitude was in
error and that Cape Cod was the feature in dispute. [29]

Less difference of opinion is noted in the association of the
bay as Penobscot Bay. Because the coast east of it lacked anything sizable enough to be conceived as the Bay of Fundy, it is
sometimes argued, not convincingly, to be this body of water.
While modifications of the bay on later Homem maps reinforced the
claim that Fundy rather than Penobscot was intended, the bay's
north-south axis was an incorrect orientation for Fundy and becomes even more unacceptable in the context of the usual apology
of magnetic error for the coast's east-west alignment. If the
Ribero coast is adjusted to its proper northeast-southwest course,
the bay is turned even further from Fundy's correct orientation.
Identification of the large bay as Penobscot also supports the claim
that the peninsula was Cape Cod.

An early modification of the features on the Ribero maps is
presumed to have been done by his successor as cosmographer,
Alonso de Chaves. On the latter's lost chart the triangular shape
in which Ribero drew the peninsula was altered to a rectangular
form. Why such a change was instituted is unknown, but it did not
increase the accuracy of the chart, since Cape Cod does not resemble a rectangle. Among the maps which retained the basic Ribero
coast but with the Chaves style peninsula were the Harleian 1536,
Desceliers 1541, Medina 1545, Gutierre 1550, Musis 1554, Darinel
1555, le Testu 1566, and Mercator's 1541 globe. Note that the
adoption of this change was more characteristic of French cartography than of Spanish or Portuguese. Many of these maps also
showed a narrower gulf between the peninsula and bay than was on
the Ribero maps, perhaps another characteristic introduced by

---

[29] Sauer suggests Cape May for the Arenas cape and the Hudson River for the Gamas
stream. See Sauer, Carl O., Sixteenth Century North America (Berkeley: University of
California Press, 1971), pp. 67-68.

Chaves.[30]

Santa Cruz showed the peninsula in a style somewhere between the outlines of his predecessors,[31] and assigned the _Arenas_ name only to its southern promontory. He provided an important clue to the identity of the bay by placing a large island south of the mainland immediately west of Cape Breton, probably intended to be present day Nova Scotia, an alteration which supports the interpretation that Ribero's bay was not Fundy. By Santa Cruz' time the Ribero bay was called Rio de las Gamas, the name by which it was most frequently labelled on sixteenth century charts and maps.

The contrast between the Santa Cruz treatment of the coast from the Rio de las Gamas to Cape Breton and the same area as shown on the maps by the Portuguese Homems illustrates the problems of untraveled cartographers trying to depict reality from the New World reports available to them. Both Spanish and Portuguese cartographers had received new information on the area from sources not totally known to us. Cartier, the only official explorer prior to the appearance of these maps, was an unlikely source because he did not sail southwest of Cape Breton. Although the Portuguese might have had the results of the Fagundes voyage at hand, it remains unanswered why his evidence took forty years to be illustrated on his countrymen's maps.[32] Unofficial voyages such as the English ones in 1527 and 1536 might have yielded some data, or the fishermen frequenting the northwest Atlantic might have supplied them.[33] Whatever the information and whatever the

---

[30]Stokes, I. N. Phelps, The Iconography of Manhattan Island (New York: Robert H. Dodd, 1916), Vol. II, pp. 22-23, 39-40.

[31]Dahlgren, E. W., Map of Santa Cruz (Stockholm: Swedish Staff-General, 1892), p. 18, claimed that Santa Cruz and Chaves maps were identical. My interpretation differs also from that of Hoffman, op. cit., p. 122, who classifies the two together, because the concern here is only with a small portion of the map, not its entire characteristics.

[32]Patterson, George, "The Portuguese on the North-East Coast of America, and the First European Attempt at Colonization There: A Lost Chapter in American History," Transactions of the Royal Society of Canada (1890), Section II, 127-73; Ganong, op. cit., pp. 46-47, 67-72; Hoffman, op. cit., pp. 33-35.

[33]In the absence of known sources of cartographic data fishermen are often assumed to be the sources. On the other hand whenever data were lacking or incorrect, the non-communicative habits of the fishermen about their fishing areas are invoked. See Purchas, Samuel, Hakluytus Posthumus or Purchas His Pilgrimes (New York: AMS Press, 1965),

sources, Santa Cruz and the Homems interpreted them differently and illustrated them in styles unique to each.

The Homem maps utilized the Ribero style coast from the southern peninsula to the small cape at the western entrance of the bay and retained the approximate latitudes of those features. But the bay or estuary was widened into a broad northward extending gulf.[34] To some the new gulf was the first appearance of the Bay of Fundy on maps, but the channel between the mainland and the Island of St. John on the earlier Santa Cruz maps is probably more deserving of that distinction. If one looks at the outline of the coast without the preconception that the new gulf was Fundy, its western shore could appear to resemble the outline of the New England coast without any significant cape at its southern end. But the entire land mass around the gulf is not only too large to be Fundy's shores but also has an incorrect axis. This interpretation further disputes the association of the Ribero cape as Cape Cod and gives weight to the arguments that it was a more southerly promontory. At the northern end of the new gulf the Homems further confused the issue. On some of their maps the gulf was linked directly with the Gulf of St. Lawrence, a situation which made the land to the east a large island. On others an isthmus was drawn between the two gulfs. Whether one accepts the interpretation of the Homem gulf to be either the Gulf of Maine as here proposed or the Bay of Fundy, their maps gave an image of the New England coast which was less satisfactory than the Ribero style. Their style was not widely copied, although some influence may be seen on the Ortelius world map of 1564.[35]

The Ribero style coast, often with some modifications, persisted into the seventeenth century, especially in Spanish cartography where it became an inbred stereotype which resisted change.

Vol. XIV, pp. 304-5, and Hoffman, op. cit., pp. 187-88, for the Rut and Hore voyages. An older interpretation of them is found in Kohl, J. G., History of the Discovery of Maine, Vol. I of "Documentary History of the State of Maine," Collections of the Maine Historical Society, 2nd Series (Portland: Bailey and Noyes, 1869), pp. 281ff. and 337ff.

[34] See Cortesão and da Mota, op. cit., Vol. II, for reproductions of the Homem maps.

[35] Koeman, C., The History of Abraham Ortelius and His Theatrum Orbis Terrum (Lausanne: Sequoia S.A., 1964), p. 14.

The bay appeared with various dimensions, sometimes a bay, otherwise as an estuary with one or more rivers entering it. Where it was called the River of Norembega, French nomenclature was used. Another example of French influence was the style which used the Ribero coast combined with the Verazzano sea and isthmus. Among the maps where that image of the area was depicted were Desceliers 1544, Lok 1582, the Carta Marina of the 1561 Ptolemy, and Gastaldi's Carta Marina 1548. Because the Verazzano sea and isthmus were supposedly sighted well south of the latitude of Cape Cod these maps have been evidence that C. de Arenas was an exaggeration of a cape at lower latitudes. However, if we accept the premise that the isthmus as located on the Verazzano map began about 40° north, the amalgamation of the two styles was logical, if highly inaccurate.[36]

The Verazzano style of the New England coast began with a voyage made earlier than the Gomez one, but it is here treated in second order because it did not have the dominant influence on cartographic traditions as did the Ribero style. In 1524 Verazzano piloted a French ship northward along the Atlantic coast from approximately Cape Fear to Cape Breton, a track paralleling in part the Gomez route.[37] On return to France Verazzano sent a description of the voyage to Francis I. Shortly after the letter was dispatched the king was defeated and captured at Pavia by Charles V, the patron of Gomez and Ribero. The original letter is lost, but its text exists in five later copies. One version was included in Ramusio's Viaggi and was translated into English for inclusion in Hakluyt's Principall Navigations;[38] another with an often meaningless text is the Florentine copy; a third is the Roman

---

[36]Wroth, op. cit., p. 167.

[37]For the conclusion that Verazzano was the pilot not the captain of the ship, see Habert, Jacques, When New York Was Called Angoulême (New York: Transocean Press, 1949), p. 23. An old interpretation which branded the evidence and voyage as fraud was in Murphy, H. C., The Voyage of Verrazzano (New York: n.p., 1875). For arguments that the voyage occurred consult Ganong, op. cit., pp. 99ff.; Harrisse, op. cit., pp. 214-28; and Wroth, op. cit.

[38]Hakluyt, Richard, The Principal Navigations Voyages Traffiques & Discoveries of the English Nation (Glasgow: James MacLehose and Sons, 1904), Vol. VIII, pp. 423-38; Ramusio, Giovanni, Terzo Volvme delle Navigationi et Viaggi.... (Venice: Stamperia de Givnti, 1556).

version, now in the J. P. Morgan Library, and is the text used for this study.[39]

The handwriting of the Roman version is in two scripts. The main text is written in a refined, highly legible style, while the marginal notes are in a different, crude style. The place names used on the map are found in the notes rather than the main text, but they are placed so that they may be readily interpolated. Wroth's study ascribes the notes to Verazzano himself. Such notes with the place names are not on any other copy of the letter.[40]

Only the northern part of the voyage concerns us here. After a brief stop at Angoulême, usually assumed to be New York harbor, the ship sailed eastward, passed a triangular shaped island about the size of Rhodes and entered a broad bay dotted with islands near one of which it anchored. These features were probably respectively Block Island, Narragansett Bay, Rhode Island, and Newport harbor. The large triangular island was named Luisa in honor of the king's mother, Louise of Savoy, regent during his captivity; however, on many maps it was erroneously called Claudia for his deceased wife. The pleasant bay and harbor were appropriately labelled Refugio. Having revictualled there, the ship continued eastward where it encountered the Armellini shoals, which are assumed to be the waters around Cape Cod. After a change of course to the north a promontory named Pallavicino, or the northern end of Cape Cod, was sighted. Somewhere along the northern coast a landing was made. Hostile natives tried to prevent a disembarkation.[41]

---

[39] Cogswell, Joseph G. (trans.), "The Voyage of John de Verazzano along the Coast of North America from Carolina to Newfoundland A. D. 1524," Collections of the New York Historical Society, 2nd Series, I (1841), 37-67; the Italian text of the Rome version and a reproduction of the map are in Colombo-Vespucci-Verazzano (Turin: L'Unione Tipografico-Editrice Torinese, 1966). The same text with an English translation is in Bacchiani, Alessandro, "Giovanni da Verazzano and His Discoveries in North America 1524," Annual Report of the American Scenic and Historic Preservation Society, XV (1910), 135-226. The Rome version, known as the Cèllere Codex, is also reprinted, transcribed, and translated in Wroth, op. cit., pp. 96-143. Wroth has a brief description of each of the five versions, pp. 93-95.

[40] Wroth, op. cit., p. 145.

[41] The natives who were considered to be uncouth and barbarous were encountered somewhere along the Maine coast which was called "Land of the Bad People." See Bacchiani, op. cit., p. 196. The Frenchmen's reception there and at Refugio were so dis-

The earliest cartographic view of the voyage was the "Maggiolo 1525" map. Better known is the planisphere done in 1529 by Verazzano's brother and known as the Verazzano map (Figure 5).[42] The coast as portrayed on it and described in the Roman text is here called the Verazzano style of the New England coast. In contrast to the Ribero North American coast where the two most distinctive features have been interpreted to be part of New England, the most prominent features, to the modern eye, on the Verazzano map were to the south. They were the isthmus and western sea beyond it. In later decades these features were sometimes shifted northward in latitude, especially after Spanish explorations such as de Soto's proved that they did not exist at the latitudes stated in the letter. If the latitude shift was high enough as on the Lok map, these characteristics became a part of the New England image.

As depicted on the Verazzano map the New England coast lies on a southwest-northeast axis from Cape Breton to the Armellini shoals. The distance between these two points accounts for nearly half of the map's total North American coast line. The line had many small indentations but only one large bay, located a short distance north of the shoals.[43] It might represent the "baia" where Verazzano encountered the hostile natives, and although islands were absent, it might be synonymous with the Rio de las Gamas of the Ribero image. The Armellini shoals extend eastward from the mainland and were shown in a dotted pattern found nowhere else along this coast, except near Florida.[44] The symbol is interpreted to mean something less than terra firma. Whether or not it included just the shoal laden waters or these waters plus nearby low lying land such as Cape Cod, Martha's Vineyard, and Nantucket can

---

similar that some scholars think that the northern Indians had been brutally treated by Europeans before Verazzano arrived. Perhaps some unknown fishermen created mayhem among them as did later Hudson's crew.

[42] See Ganong, op. cit., pp. 99-133, for a discussion of the map.

[43] There was no comparable indentation on the Maggiolo version.

[44] The pattern was also found around the Bahamas and some of the West Indian islands. On the reproduction of the Maggiolo map in Harrisse, op. cit., plate X, the pattern appeared only at the shoals.

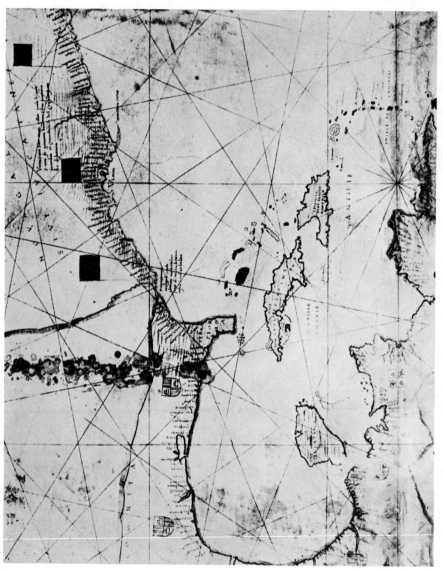

Fig. 5.--The Verazzano Style: A Portion of the Verazzano Planisphere (courtesy of the Yale University Press)

not be determined from either the map or the letter. West of the
Armellini shoals the Verazzano coast arced northwestward to
Refugio-Luisa and then curved southwestward to Florida. The
island Luisa was placed at the entrance to the Refugio bay and was
the only island along the coast.[45]

The influence of the Verazzano style of the New England coast
on later cartography was noticeably less than that of the Ribero
image. However, the nomenclature of the map and the Roman letter did appear in diverse forms on many Italian maps where French
sources in some distorted form were widely used. How much the
gradual discrediting of the Verazzano isthmus and sea played in a
general distrust of the map's other features is not known, but it
may be assumed that a relationship existed.

An early alteration of the Ribero style into something more
closely approximating the real coast was a style marked by the portrayal of the northeastern section of mid-latitude North America
as a massive eastward projecting peninsula (Figure 6). Such a portrayal was inherent to the Ribero image, if the Arenas cape was
either omitted or reduced in size. While the resultant coastline
often lacked large indentations, on some maps there was a large
stream or estuary which was a modification of the Ribero bay.
Slightly north of 40° north these coasts had an east-west axis which
continued for several degrees of longitude and then turned north-
northeast to Cape Breton. The greater reality of a northeast massive peninsula with proper orientation must be balanced against the
loss of anything which resembled the major features of the coast
such as Cape Cod, the Maine gulf, or the offshore islands as one
could find in the Ribero style. Because this altered style was
used most frequently on world or hemisphere maps, it was inevita-
bly associated with very small scale, a reason perhaps for the
omission of detail. But the argument is not totally valid because
the Rasciotti 1583 map depicted details of islands, capes, and bays.
Although maps of several nationalistic schools of cartography contained examples of this type of coast, its greatest currency was in

---

[45]There were considerable differences between the Maggiolo and Verazzano maps for
this section of the coast. On the former the southwest trend of the coast continued, a situation which gave a long distance between the shoals and Refugio. Luisa was placed slightly
west of the entrance to Refugio.

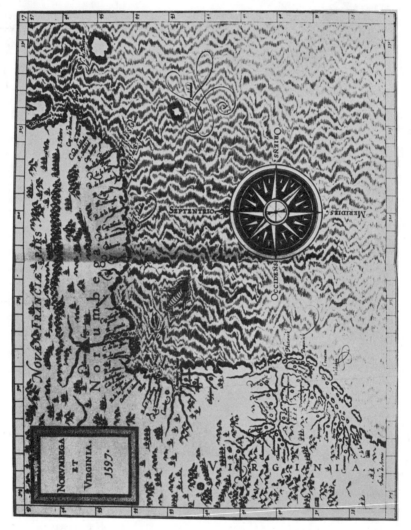

Fig. 6. --The Modified Ribero Style: Wytfliet's Map of Norembega

the works of Mercator and Ortelius. Unfortunately it continued to reappear in editions of their atlases long after accurate maps of the coast were available.[46]

Italian Style

Italian cartographers of the sixteenth century rarely had direct access to the accumulating data from the New World. But they were keenly interested in such information and sought it from the nations active in the New World exploration.[47] However, because they received reports second or third hand, such reality as those reports might have contained often were distorted and further warped when the Italian map makers blended the materials together. Some of the Italian cartographers chose not to work within the Ribero or Verazzano traditions, and they produced a distinctive, imaginative, but highly unrealistic image of the New England coast. The principal characteristics of the Italianate style were (1) a mixing of features from French and Spanish sources, (2) total scale distortion of the coastal features, and (3) a coastline distinguished by numerous embayments and peninsulas which seem to have no counterpart in reality (Figures 7 and 8).

Two groups of sixteenth century Italian maps are used here to illustrate this image. One group is maps which portrayed the entire eastern coast of North America as well as large portions of the continent,[48] while on the second group only the northeastern

---

[46]Large scale use of this image may be seen in Wytfliet, Cornelius à, Descriptionis Ptolemaicae Augmentum (Louvain: J. Boogaard, 1597), sheet entitled "Norvmbega et Virginia 1597." In Bagrow, op. cit., p. 134, is a facsimile of Mercator's 1538 version of the image. A reproduction of Ortelius' use of the image in his Theatrum (1590) is in Skelton, R. A., Decorative Printed Maps of the 15th to 18th Centuries (London: Spring Books, 1952), plate XV. The Rasciotti 1583 map is reproduced in Remarkable Maps of the 15th, 16th, 17th Centuries (Amsterdam: Frederik Muller & Co., 1894), Vol. I, plate 12. A German example is Frans Hogenberg, "Americae et Proximarum Regionum orae descriptio" (1589).

[47]The numerous maps of this period which survive in Italian archives and libraries are only one evidence of the Italian Renaissance curiosity and collection of New World materials.

[48]The true nature of the continentality of North America was not known when these maps were made, and they reveal the ideas which were held on this topic. Gastaldi (1546) and Forlani depicted North America as a large eastward extension of Asia. Zaltieri separated North America from Asia by a Strait of Anian. Camocio avoided the problem by not showing the western part of the land mass.

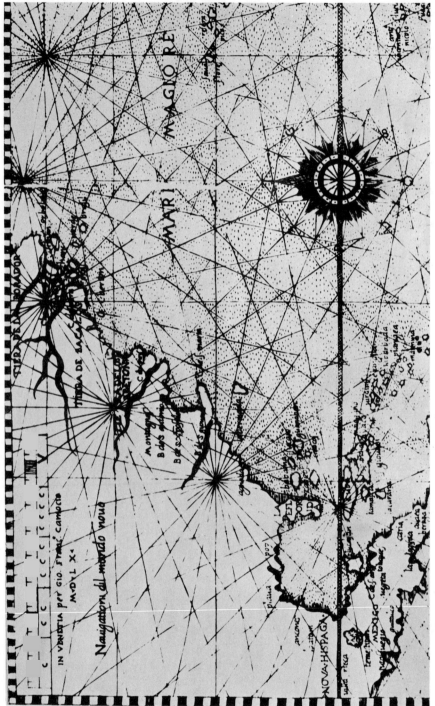

Fig. 7.--The Italian Style: A Portion of Camocio's World Map of 1560 (courtesy of the Library of Congress)

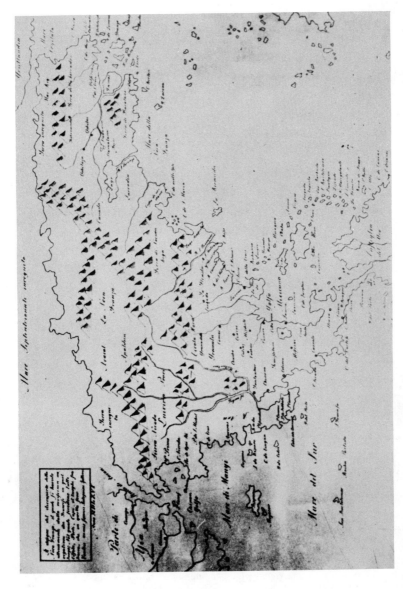

Fig. 8. --The Italian Style: Zaltieri's North American Map of 1566 (courtesy of the Library of Congress)

mid-latitude part of the coast was shown. From the first group
five maps are the bases of discussion: Gastaldi's 1546 world map,
his 1548 "della Terra Nova del Bacalaos," Camocio's 1560 world
map, Forlani's 1565 world map, and Zaltieri's 1566 North America
map.[49]

The orientation of the east coast on the first group of maps
was a southwest-northeast axis. But on the Gastaldi and Forlani
maps the coastline had the traditional distance of east-west axis
before reaching Cape Breton. That pattern was repeated on the
Zaltieri map but with an east-west segment of greater length, a
feature which resembled the stylized east-west coast on the late
Ribero image maps. Each of these coastlines had numerous indentations, but the largest one was usually a reduced version of the
Ribero gulf from the Arenas cape to the smaller cape of many
islands. Its latitude was 40° north plus or minus a few degrees so
that its placement also corresponded to the Ribero original. The
slender Ribero style peninsula was used, but it was called C. de
S. Maria on each of these maps. The reduced gulf had at its northern end a small cape which in outline duplicated the Ribero C. de
muchas islas, but only on the Zaltieri version did it have a comparable name, C. de molte isole. Beyond that cape where the Ribero
bay or estuary should be, each of these Italian maps showed a large
river estuary with a stream draining from the continent's interior.
On the second Gastaldi map the area north of the estuary was labelled "larcadia," northeast of which were other Verazzano place
names. The "larcadia" name was repeated on the Forlani and
Zaltieri maps, but the other Verazzano nomenclature was omitted.
Only the Zaltieri map retained the insular features of the coast as
drawn in the Ribero image. The loss of that characteristic seems
somewhat inexplicable because of the general Spanish influence
observable on these maps.

---

[49] The Gastaldi world map was originally published in Venice in 1546; it is reproduced
in Remarkable Maps . . . , Vol. IV. His later "della Terra Nova del Bacalaos" is in the
1548 Venice edition of Ptolemy's Geografia. Camocio's map was produced at Venice in
1560; a negative of the original in the Map Division of the Library of Congress was consulted for this study. Paulo Forlani made his world map in 1565 either at Venice or
Verona; it is also reproduced in Remarkable Maps . . . , Vol. IV. The Zaltieri map is
part of the Kohl Collection in the Library of Congress and may also be found in Lafréry,
Antoine, Geografia tavole moderne di geografia (Rome, 1575).

The Forlani and Zaltieri maps contained data from the Cartier voyages. Sadly their inclusion did not increase the accuracy of the maps but rather complicated the already distorted image. On both of these maps a large interior lake represented the rumors of such bodies told to Cartier. Neither cartographer, however, associated it correctly with the river which Cartier explored; Forlani left it isolated, while Zaltieri added a new river, S. Lorenzo, to connect with a small arm of the Atlantic called "Mare della Nova Franza."

It is impossible to identify real coastal features from the depictions on these Italian maps. Unfortunately such accuracies as the Ribero or Verazzano style contained were lost when the Italian armchair traveler-cartographers attempted to reconcile the conflicting aspects of them or added new data.

Maps of the second group had many of the same characteristics and hence limitations of the first group, but the former shows us the Italian conception of coastal details lacking from the larger maps. A Gastaldi 1550 map of Norembega and an anonymous 1560 one of New France are used to discuss these features (Figure 9).[50] Both had a coast on an east-west axis. While the Gastaldi one was an Italian impression exclusively of Verazzano data, the 1560 sheet combined French and Spanish materials. Both coastlines contained numerous small embayments, all fairly uniform in size. The 1560 map illustrates the extreme of nonselectivity to be found among the Italian cartographers of the time. Instead of combining comparable phenomena into a single map feature, they were indiscriminately duplicated, a circumstance which produced a grotesquely enlarged coastline. For example, the Ribero style Arenas cape was placed south and west of another large peninsula called C. de S. Maria, the usual Italian name for Arenas itself. In proper association to the Arenas cape was the equivalent of the Ribero bay and cape of many islands, but they appeared again elsewhere on the map. French materials were also distorted. While Norembega was the interior tributary to the Ribero gulf, Arcadia became only a large peninsula

---

[50]The Gastaldi Norembega map appeared in Ramusio's Viaggi (1556), Vol. III. A reproduction of it is in Taylor, E. G. R. (ed.), The Original Writings and Correspondence of the Two Richard Hakluyts (London: Hakluyt Society, 1935), Vol. I, p. 174. The anonymous Italian map is plate 13 of Remarkable Maps . . . , Vol. I.

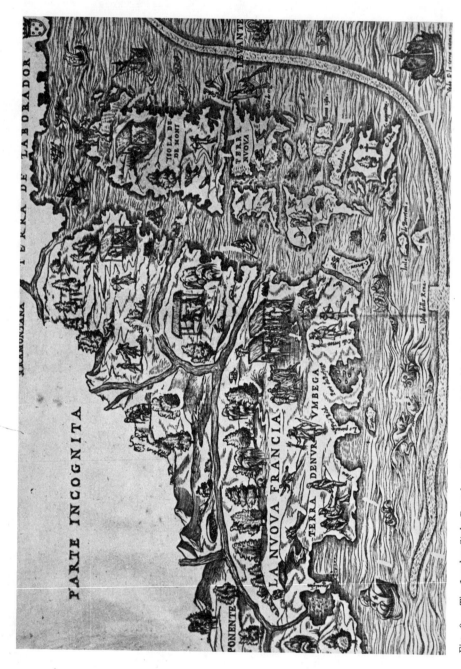

Fig. 9.--The Insular Style Based on Verazzano and Cartier Data: Gastaldi's 1550 Map of New France (courtesy of the Map Division, The New York Public Library, Astor, Lenox and Tilden Foundations).

near the mouth of a river draining from a large Cartier inspired lake. That river was labelled both S. Lorenzo and Rio grande, the latter being a name sometimes used for the Rio de las Gamas, the bay of the Ribero image. The drawer/compiler obviously thought inclusiveness to be a cartographic virtue, but the resultant image was so confused that it, like the maps of the first Italian group, is worthless to argue modern associations of the coastal configuration.

New England as an Island

During the second year of the Plymouth colony's existence Robert Cushman, a sometime agent for the colony, reminded his listeners that New England was an island. Later founders of the Puritan colony concurred in this belief, and it appeared in print as late as 1672.[51] To any challenge of the validity of the insular concept impeccable English cartographic evidence could have been offered as proof of the claim. From the half century preceding the Pilgrims' settlement, no less than six of the surviving English maps portrayed this part of the North American continent as a large island.[52] Two of these maps were associated with the famous Elizabethan adventurer, Sir Humphrey Gilbert, whose role in English images will be discussed in the next chapter. Michael Lok's map of 1582 used the insular image (Figure 10), and closer to the date of Cushman's sermon were the Hakluyt-Wright map of 1599 and the Molineaux map of 1600. The Velasco map of circa

---

[51]Cushman, Robert, The First Sermon Ever Preached in New England (New York: J. E. D. Comstock, 1858), p. xi. Edward Winslow affirmed the insular concept in his Good News from New England (London: William Bladen and John Bellamie, 1624), reprinted in Arber, E. (ed.), The Story of the Pilgrim Fathers (London: Ward and Downey, 1897), pp. 592-93. John Humfrey and Emmanuel Downing were two Puritan leaders who held the concept. See Winthrop Papers (Boston: Massachusetts Historical Society, 1931), Vol. II, pp. 325, 333. The belief was stated by William Wood in his promotional New-Englands Prospect (London: Tho. Cotes and John Bellamie, 1634), reprinted in Young, Alexander (ed.), Chronicles of the First Planters of the Colony of Massachusetts Bay (Boston: Charles C. Little and James Brown, 1846), pp. 391-92. A later statement of the belief was Josselyn, John, New Englands Rarities (London: G. Widdowes, 1672), in Archaeologia Americana, IV (1860), 140. Also consult Bradford, William, History of Plymouth Plantation 1620-1647 (Boston: Massachusetts Historical Society, 1912), Vol. I, p. 270.

[52]Of important late Elizabethan maps of the New World only the Dee map of 1580 and Thomas Hood's map of 1592 did not use the insular style. Both showed the coast in the continental Ribero image. For the Hood map see Kunstmann, op. cit., Blatt XIII.

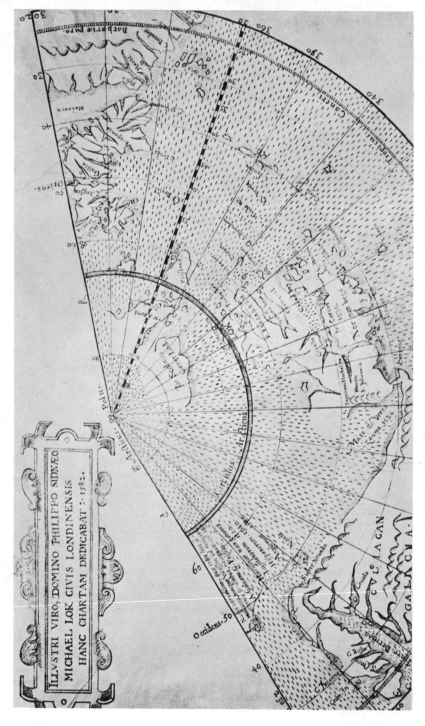

Fig. 10. --The Insular Style Combining Ribero and Verazzano Elements: A Portion of Lok's 1582 Map of the New World (courtesy of the Map Division, The New York Public Library, Astor, Lenox and Tilden Foundations).

1610 was a significant example of fact and fancy still found on maps of its time, for the Atlantic coast on it is the oldest survival of a realistic style. It had a New England detached from the mainland. However, it is doubtful that such maps were a major influence on the thinking of the early English settlers. The maps reported the belief rather than inspired it. The conception of the Velasco map is also found in reports contemporaneous to Pilgrim and Puritan settlement wherein the Hudson River was linked to the St. Lawrence.[53]

While the above mentioned maps and charts proved that the insular style was an accepted image in English North American cartography between 1570 and 1610, the English were not the innovators of the image but had adopted it from earlier continental cartographers. The early sixteenth century treatment of northwest Atlantic discoveries as islands might have been an influence in the origin of the image, but there is no substantial evidence to link directly the two insular images. Gastaldi's use of the style for New England on his 1550 Norembega map is one of the earliest examples of the concept which had its beginnings in the information coming from French sources. He linked the southward flowing streams identified from the Verazzano voyage with the large east-west flowing river explored by Cartier. Ruscelli's 1561 New World map used the same materials to get a depiction comparable to Gastaldi's. Another misconception of the Cartier data accentuated the river's long estuary and drew it too sharply to the southwest so that New England was connected to the mainland only by a narrow isthmus.[54]

Another source of the insular style was an interpretation of the large Ribero bay as a strait between Cartier's river and the Atlantic, perhaps to document the existence of a northwest passage. An early example of this error may be seen on the "Callopoda

---

[53] Winthrop Papers, Vol. II, loc. cit.

[54] The Gastaldi map has been discussed here in the section on the Italian image. Ruscelli's map was reproduced in Winsor, Justin, "Maps of the Eastern Coast of North America," in Winsor, J. (ed.), Narrative and Critical History of America (Boston: Houghton Mifflin, 1884), Vol. IV, p. 92. Examples of the last misconception may be seen on Teixeira 1573 map in Cortesão and da Mota, op. cit., Vol. II, plate 28, and the "Harleian Mappemonde" (c. 1536-37).

Portalan" (Venice, 1550) where the Gamas stream was connected to
the St. Lawrence. The work of the Portuguese cartographer Vaz
Dourado illustrated the confusion which existed among map makers.
In his 1568 atlas he drew the bay as a strait, but in 1571 he abandoned that style in favor of the older, more prevalent Ribero style
for the river. But continuing uncertainty of the validity of the
insular concept was demonstrated by Lasso's use of the insular
image in his 1590 atlas.[55] Among northern cartographers the low-
lander Hondius in 1590 also showed the Ribero river as a strait.
Although the Hakluyt-Wright map had Atlantic coastal features
which do not fit the main images of this study, the insularity of
New England on it was the result of a long, narrow strait drawn on
a northwest-southeast axis between the Canadian river and the
Atlantic, a situation shown earlier on the Lok map and the 1582
Gilbert polar map. The Velasco map also belongs to the riverine
strait tradition, but on it the strait was a combination of the Hud-
son and Richelieu rivers and Lake Champlain being linked to the
St. Lawrence.

A final and less certain treatment of New England as an island
was on the Homem maps. There the area east of the great gulf was
sometimes detached at the northeastern end of the gulf by a strait
connecting to the Gulf of St. Lawrence. Whether or not this depiction represents an example of New England's insular concept de-
pends on acceptance or rejection of the Homem gulf as the Bay of
Fundy.

Realistic Style

The realistic style is one in which the coast is portrayed as
it would appear on a modern map. Two groups of maps attained a
realistic portrayal of the coast before 1620: the French maps of
Champlain and the English Velasco and Smith maps.[56]

---

[55]Cortesão and da Mota, op. cit., Vol. III, plates 370 and 378.

[56]In the decade 1610-19 the Dutch developed a realistic cartographic image of the
southern New England coast from Cape Cod west to New York harbor, but in spite of
Adrian Block's visit to the northern coast their treatment of it remained below the stan-
dards of Champlain and the English map makers. See "New Netherland, Dutch 1616" in
Winsor, J. (comp.), The Kohl Collection (Washington: Government Printing Office, 1904),
p. 94.

Champlain was the first major explorer of the New England coast to convert himself the data which he gathered into maps.[57] Before he established the focus of French North American settlement in the St. Lawrence valley, he participated in French attempts to put fur trading sites along the northern New England coast. It was in that period of his life when he made three journeys along the New England coast; on his longest trip he went to the south side of Cape Cod. In addition to a series of small large-scale charts of the harbors into which he entered, his explorations were the sources of data for three small-scale maps which were accurate enough to be classified among the first realistic maps of the coast.[58]

The oldest of the maps was a 1607 sheet which showed only the Atlantic coast from Cape Cod to Nova Scotia.[59] The later ones, dated 1612 and 1613, showed all of what was then considered to be New France. Although the 1613 map was probably the most accurate for the coastal outline, there was curiously no progressive increase of the maps' realism with the dates of construction, for the 1612 one was in many features the least accurate. All of them were grossly inadequate south of Cape Cod, where Champlain did not travel.

The 1607 map was also closest to Champlain's experience on the New England coast, and in spite of some inaccuracies his depictions of its features gave on this map an individuality to its peninsulas, bays, and islands lacking on earlier maps. He intertwined characteristics of earlier cartographic images with the results of his personal knowledge. For example, the general curve of the coast was reminiscent of the Ribero style and the shape of Cape Cod was a Chaves style. While the V shaped mouth of the Norembega river resembled its form on many previous charts, Champlain's

---

[57] The reports of other explorers had been the primary sources for cartographers-- notably Gomez for Ribero and Verazzano for his brother. Champlain and Smith share the singular distinction of being both map maker and explorer of the coast. Their direct experience with the area was a critical factor in displacing the cartographic misconceptions which had become stylized for the region.

[58] Reproductions of his maps and charts as well as the text of his journals are in Voyages of Samuel de Champlain (Boston: Prince Society, 1880), 3 vols.

[59] Original in the Library of Congress, Map Division. The 7 was written over an 8 in the date. It is not known if the change was made by Champlain or was a later alteration.

peninsulas and island-dotted bay left no doubt that it can be only
Penobscot Bay. As the link between the realistic image based on
personal knowledge and traditions of earlier images, Champlain
here resolved the question of which estuary was intended for the
Ribero bay and the River of Norembega of earlier maps. Passamaquoddy Bay also appeared on this map for the first time in recognizable form. His portrayal of the Kennebec estuary as a bay was
an error, but his placement of the stream's mouth north of Cape
Cod was correct as was his drawing of Casco Bay and its islands.

The New England coast on Champlain's 1612 map of New
France retrogressed from the accuracy level of the 1607 chart.[60]
This probably was the result of problems created by joining his
New England data with the more recently acquired knowledge of the
St. Lawrence and interior regions. For example, the St. Lawrence
was placed on an east-west axis and much of New England drawn
parallel to it so that the latter had the improper orientation of
many prior styles. The correct 1607 longitudinal relationship
between Cape Cod and the Maine coast disappeared, as the Maine
coast was distorted too far eastward. The placement of Lake
Champlain too near the coast illustrated the problems of proper
relationships between the coast and its hinterland. While Penobscot and Passamaquoddy bays retained appearances comparable to
their 1607 versions, the estuary of the Kennebec was distorted by
the omission of one of the streams draining into it. Cape Cod was
not drawn in the Chaves style, but it was no closer to the reality
than in 1607, and the area south of it was still fanciful. Latitude
was also grossly misconceived, for Nova Scotia was put on the
same parallel as Cape Cod, with the resultant Gulf of Maine being
reminiscent of the gulf on the Homem maps.

The 1613 map was on such small scale that many details on
the previous two maps disappeared, but in general outline and
proper orientation it was the best of the three (Figure 11). It

---

[60] A comparable assessment may be made of the New England section of Lescarbot's
1609 map of New France (Winsor, Kohl Collection, p. 68). The general curve of the coast
resembled Champlain's 1607 version, but the details were so inaccurate as to question
Lescarbot's judgment in assessing Champlain's work. The Lescarbot map was most like
Champlain's between Cape Cod and the mouth of the Kennebec where Champlain was inaccurate; the accuracy with which Champlain had outlined the northern portion of the coast was
not repeated by Lescarbot.

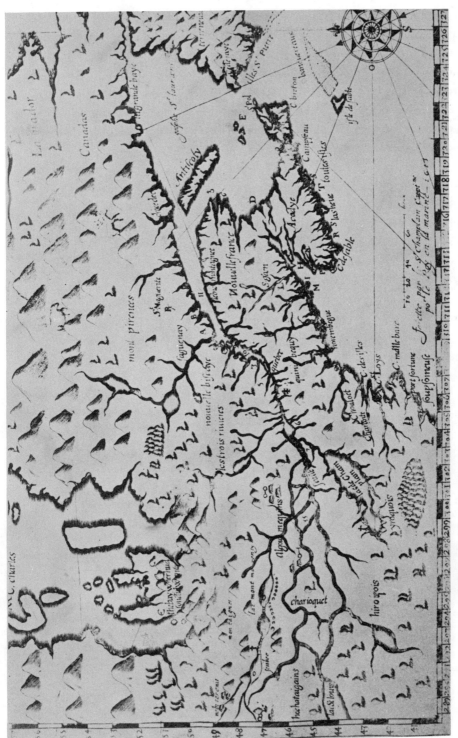

Fig. 11.—The Realistic Style: The New England Section of Champlain's 1613 Map of New France

retained distortions such as the unrecognizable Cape Cod and the oversized peninsulas of Massachusetts Bay. However, its latitudes and longitudes were for the most part correct. A proper northeast curve of the coast from Massachusetts Bay to the Bay of Fundy appeared here for the first time on Champlain's cartography. His treatment of the Kennebec was superior to those of 1607 and 1612 but suffered in all versions from inadequate knowledge of the drainage pattern of that part of Maine.

Antedating the last Champlain map by some three years, the so-called Velasco map of circa 1610 is the oldest known map to give a realistic outline of the eastern coast of the United States (Figure 12).[61] The map was discovered in the Archives of Simancas, Spain, and first published in 1890. The date and circumstances of construction and sources of data are not totally known.[62] The Virginia sector resembled the maps of John White and John Smith, whose works were probably used by the unknown cartographer.[63] The presence of certain place names--i.e. Elizabeth's Isles, Whitson's Head and Bay, and the Isle of St. George--indicates that the compiler knew of the English voyages to the New England coast in the first decade of the seventeenth century. French place names in northern Maine, the Bay of Fundy, and Nova Scotia as well as stylistic duplications suggest familiarity with Champlain's activities in those regions. The striking similarity between the Penobscot area on this map and Champlain's 1607 map

---

[61]Of the New England section only the coast between Buzzards Bay and the Hudson River had serious omissions or distortions. Narragansett Bay was incomplete, and the Verazzano isle of Claudia (Luisa) reappeared. Long Island was drawn as a part of the mainland, and Nantucket was omitted.

[62]Brown, Alexander, The Genesis of the United States (New York: Russell & Russell, 1964 [reprint of 1890 edition]), Vol. I, pp. 457-61, where a reproduction of the map faces p. 456. Skelton, Explorers' Maps, p. 270, calls it the Velasco map after the Spanish ambassador who probably sent it to Philip III of Spain. It is discussed in Stokes, op. cit., Vol. II, pp. 51ff., and there reproduced in color. It is also reproduced as plate 42 in Wroth, op. cit. A comparison of the Velasco map and the earlier Virginia Company map (circa 1606-8) shows the realistic status of knowledge of the former in contrast to the latter's misconceptions which included the use of the stylistic Ribero bay as New York harbor. See Stokes, op. cit., Vol. II, pp. 49-51 and plate 21A for the Virginia Company map.

[63]Lorant, Stefan, The New World (New York: Duell, Sloan, & Pearce, 1946), pp. 186-87.

45

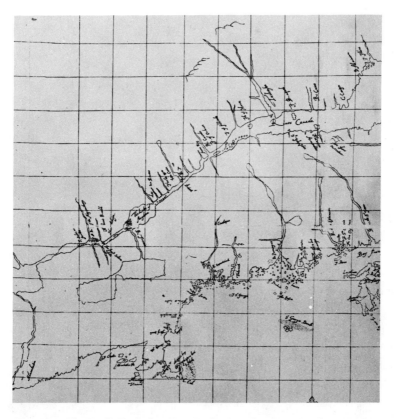

Fig. 12.--The Realistic Style: New England on the c. 1610 Velasco Map (courtesy of the Library of Congress).

more than hints that French materials were incorporated into the
English map. But although the outlines of Penobscot Bay on these
two maps was a general V shape, the English version had enough
differing details to conclude that however much information the
Velasco drawer had from French sources, he also had independent
materials from the English voyages which were given priority over
the French whenever the two were in conflict. The drawer was
also capable of his own errors, for he added a major stream between the Kennebec and Penobscot rivers where none exists.

The superiority of English sources over the French was shown
in the accurate depiction of most of Massachusetts Bay and Cape
Cod, a situation which consistently escaped Champlain. For the
part of the coast between Cape Cod and Casco Bay the Velasco map
is the oldest surviving example of a realistic outline. Particularly
noteworthy is the accurate shape of Cape Cod which appeared here
probably for the first time in European cartography in realistic
outline. It was marred only on the south by the absence of islands
and on the west by an incomplete Narragansett Bay and the omission of Long Island Sound.

The map which resulted from John Smith's 1614 visit to the
New England coast continued the accuracy achieved on the Velasco
map, although it is not known if Smith saw the latter. Smith's map,
however, covered a smaller area because it coincided with the
area which he explored and hence included only the coast from the
northern shore of Cape Cod to Penobscot Bay (Figure 13).[64] His
treatment of details increased the accuracy of the general coastal
outline, and his portrayal of mainland topographic features, especially the Camden Hills, continued Champlain's efforts to relate
landscape content as well as coastal outlines. Unfortunately Smith
decorated his map with symbols of his settlement dreams and place
names which for the most part had no future influence. He continued the confusion about the mouth of the Kennebec by leaving the
upper end of Casco Bay open and placing a major stream just east
of that bay. With Smith's details, the major features on Champlain's map of 1613, and the coastal outline of the Velasco map the

---

[64]Arber, E. (ed.), Travels and Works of Captain John Smith (Edinburgh: John Grant, 1910), Vol. II, p. 694.

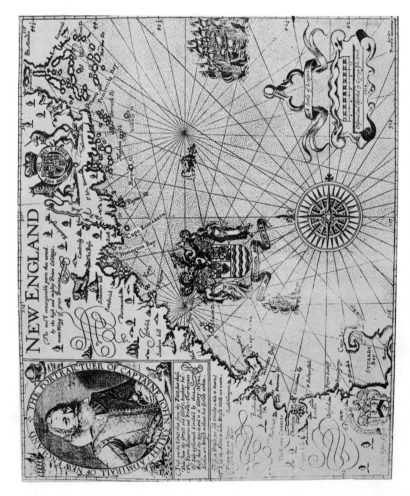

Fig. 13. --The Realistic Style: John Smith's 1616 Map of New England

modern era of New England cartography began with an accurate image of the coast. The task ahead was threefold: to displace the earlier incorrect images of the coast which still lingered on many maps, to determine the relationship of the area to the continent, and to extend accurate mapping into the interior.

CHAPTER II

GILBERT'S NOREMBEGA:

THE ELIZABETHAN IMAGE

The first English effort to colonize the eastern coast of North
America ended in 1583 with the loss of one ship on shoals south of
Newfoundland and the general despondency of the fleet's crew which
forced Sir Humphrey Gilbert, admiral of the expedition, to abandon
his course and return to England, but not before issuing a promise
to the crew that he would return another year to finish the task.[1]
On the homeward voyage Gilbert's ship sank with total loss of
hands, maps, and papers. Gilbert's role as an activist in English
colonization was assumed by his half-brother and then favorite of
the Queen, Sir Walter Raleigh, while Gilbert's proposed colony
faded into the mists of the nearly forgotten. Gilbert's scheme
remains as the first active phase of a vague Elizabethan image of
the New World which combined myth and fact into a utilitarian
vision of an earthly paradise.[2]

Behind Gilbert's venture was the Elizabethan image of some
part of the eastern North American coast as a satisfactory location for England's first American outpost. Other than the fact that
powerful Englishmen were willing to support such a scheme, most
aspects of the enterprise remain conjectures. Problematic are the
exact location and functions of the colony and the types and sources

---

[1]Hakluyt, Richard, The Principal Navigations Voyages Traffiques & Discoveries of
the English Nation (Glasgow: James MacLehose and Sons, 1904), Vol. VIII, pp. 65-69;
Quinn, D. B. (ed.), The Voyages and Colonising Enterprises of Sir Humphrey Gilbert
(London: Hakluyt Society, 1940), Vol. II, pp. 415-16. Gilbert has not had the benefit of a
recent biographer; for a competent study of his life see Gosling, W. G., The Life of Sir
Humphrey Gilbert (London: Constable & Co., 1911).

[2]Shepard, Paul, Man in the Landscape (New York: Alfred A. Knopf, 1964), pp.
48-50, discusses New World images of this type.

of information which produced the favorable image among Gilbert's backers. In this chapter the bases of the Elizabethan image, its character, and the part of the American coast to which it applied are discussed.

Scant evidence indicates that Gilbert had decided to establish his colony in Norembega. Of the few surviving records of the voyage, only Clarke's defense of his actions during the loss of the Delight had a specific reference to this location. The title of his treatise included the phrase, ". . . going to the discovery of Norembega, with Sir Humphrey Gilbert. . . ."[3] The agreement between Gilbert's associates and John Dee guaranteed to the clairvoyant doctor lands near the River of Norembega,[4] an arrangement which was concluded during Peckham's visit to Dee to determine the validity of Spanish and Portuguese titles to Norembega.[5] The ubiquitous source of fact and fiction in Elizabeth's London, Mendoza, the Spanish ambassador, informed Philip II of Spain that the chosen location was within New France and that Gilbert had sailed the northern route to Norembega.[6] Later he believed that Raleigh was preparing to follow Gilbert into Norembega.[7] Holinshed's Chronicles, compiled a few years after Gilbert's death, described the colonial site for Gilbert's two attempts: "This countrie of Norembega . . . Sir Humfrie Gilbert, brother of Sir Walter Raleigh . . . did attempt to discover, with intention to settle an

---

[3]Fuller, Thomas, The History of the Worthies of England (London: J. G. W. L. and W. G., 1662), Vol. I, p. 458; Quinn, Voyages and Colonising Enterprises, Vol. II, p. 423; and Parry, J. H., The Age of Reconnaissance (London: Weidenfeld and Nicolson, 1963), pp. 211-12.

[4]Document in British Public Record Office reprinted in Goodwin, W. B., "The Dee River of 1583 and Its Relation to Norumbega," Collections of the Rhode Island Historical Society, XXVII (January, 1934), 38-50; Mood, Fulmer, "Narragansett Bay and Dee River, 1583," Collections of the Rhode Island Historical Society, XXVIII (October, 1935), 97-100.

[5]Halliwell, James C. (ed.), The Private Diary of Dr. John Dee (London: Camden Society, 1842), p. 16.

[6]Tenison, E. M., Elizabethan England (Royal Leamington Spa: by author, 1933), Vol. IV, pp. 246-47; Quinn, Voyages and Colonising Enterprises, Vol. II, p. 364.

[7]Quinn, D. B. (ed.), The Roanoke Voyages 1584-1590 (London: Hakluyt Society, 1955), Vol. II, pp. 719, 728-29, 731.

English colonie there. . . . "[8]   Admiralty court records also identified Norembega as the location.[9]

Some contemporory materials were vague about the location
of the colony. Hayes, like Clarke a veteran of the ill-fated voyage, simply placed the colonial site in temperate climate south of
Newfoundland.[10] A petition of West Countrymen identified the
area of interest, "The Frenche haue their portion to the northe, &
directlie contrarie to that which we seke."[11]

Actions of Gilbert and his associates further identify Norembega as the area of colonial interest. Gilbert stood £500 bond for
the 1579 or 1580 reconnaissance of the Norembega coast by the
Portuguese Simon Fernandez who was also an agent of Walsingham,
the Queen's principal secretary.[12] Hakluyt's preface to Florio's
translation of the Ramusio version of Cartier's reports mentioned
Norembega and the Saguenay as potential areas of English colonization.[13] In his own Divers Voyages in which a plea for English colonization was dedicated to Sir Philip Sidney, a onetime associate
of Gilbert's schemes, Hakluyt had a section subtitled "The discouerie of Morumbega [sic],"[14] an additional evidence that the
group of expansionists who surrounded the Queen had focused their
choice on Norembega.

None of these sources, however, stated precisely what part
of eastern North America was Norembega or identified the site

---

[8]Quoted in Quinn, Voyages and Colonising Enterprises, Vol. I, p. 237.

[9]Records are reprinted in Quinn, Voyages and Colonising Enterprises, Vol. II, p. 378.

[10]Slafter, Carlos (ed.), Sir Humfrey Gylbert and His Enterprise of Colonization in America (Boston: Prince Society, 1903), pp. 113-15.

[11]Ibid., p. 234.

[12]Quinn, Voyages and Colonising Enterprises, Vol. I, p. 50, Vol. II, pp. 239-40; Read, Conyers, Mr. Secretary Walsingham and the Policy of Queen Elizabeth (New York: Archon Books, 1967 [reprint of 1925 edition]), Vol. III, pp. 389-404; Calendar of State Papers: Colonial Series (London: H. M. Stationery Office, 1860), Vol. I, p. 2.

[13]Taylor, E. G. R. (ed.), The Original Writings and Correspondence of the Two Richard Hakluyts (London: Hakluyt Society, 1935), Vol. I, p. 21; Yates, F. A., John Florio: The Life of an Italian in Shakespeare's England (Cambridge: Cambridge University Press, 1934), pp. 56-58.

[14]Hakluyt, Richard, Divers Voyages Touching the Discoverie of America (London: G. Woodcocke, 1582 [facsimile reprint Ann Arbor: University Microfilms, 1966]).

within Norembega where the colony was to be planted. On the latter issue, Hayes stated that a colonial site was not chosen before
sailing, ". . . not a certaine & determinate place of habitation
selected. . . ."[15] If Hayes were incorrect, the information was
lost with Gilbert. Or it is also possible that the final choice was
to have been made by Gilbert after a survey of the coast. But on
the basis of the detailed description of the mouth of the River of
Norembega (Penobscot) which Fernandez and Walker returned to
England,[16] it is suggested that, if not the designate site of the
colony, at least it was the planned rendezvous for the fleet after
it left Newfoundland. Additional implications that the mouth of the
Penobscot figured directly in the plans were that such a site would
be consistent with Gilbert's early hope to establish a base for
attacks on the Spanish West Indies and the persistence and tenacity
with which West Countrymen later pursued activities on the Maine
coast.[17]

Where Was Norembega?

On many mid and late sixteenth century maps and charts the
word Norembega or a variant spelling was used in three manners.
(1) It was the name for a broad expanse of territory immediately
south of Newfoundland, the Bacallaos, or the land of Cortereal as
the area at the entrance of the Gulf of St. Lawrence was variously
called. It was generally put between 40 and 50 degrees north latitude. On some of those maps Norembega was placed and so lettered
that it might be construed to be a subdivision of New France. The
Gastaldi "Norumbega" map is such an example and represents the
type of map which Mendoza viewed to argue to his king that only
French claims were about to be violated. The total area to which
the name was applied was never delimited on those maps. (2) A
large stream which drained that area was often called the River of

---

[15] Quinn, Voyages and Colonising Enterprises, Vol. II, p. 422.

[16] Calendar of State Papers, loc. cit.; De Costa, B. F., Ancient Norombega or the Voyages of Simon Ferdinando and John Walker to the Penobscot River 1579-1580 (Albany: Joel Munsell's Sons, 1890), pp. 7-8.

[17] "A Discourse How Hir Majestie May Annoy the King of Spayne," dated November 6, 1577, reprinted in Slafter, op. cit., p. 240.

Norembega, although Rio de las Gamas and Rio Grande were alter-
nates which associated the feature with the large bay of the Ribero
style of the coast. (3) A settlement of some sort depicted on the
banks of that stream was called Norembega. These uses of the
word had examples in the nomenclature of the national cartographic
schools flourishing during Gilbert's time, but only the English
usage will be considered as evidence here.

Three of the four maps associated with Gilbert's ventures
into the New World used the word in the first and third manners.
It was absent from the 1576 Gilbert map. The Lok map of 1582 and
the second Gilbert one displayed the estuary as a riverine strait,
making the area between it and the Gulf of St. Lawrence an island.
On both maps the large island was named Norembega, the only use
of the word on each.

The Dee map of 1580 was drawn in the Ribero style. Norembega was located on the Atlantic side of a mountain range symbol-
izing the drainage divide between the St. Lawrence River and the
Atlantic flowing Rio de las Gamas. The name of the stream like
the other place names along this coastal section were taken directly from Spanish sources. The vast knowledge of Spanish materials
which the map demonstrated is ample evidence why Peckham and
others consulted Dee on Spanish title to the coast. Dee also identified the settlement on the Gamas as Norembega. On the basis of
this map two interpretations of Norembega may be discarded. The
thesis that Dee considered the word synonymous with North America is untenable, for he used the term only for the northeastern
part of the United States and adjoining Canada. It has been argued
that the Dee River of his grant from Peckham was Narragansett
Bay which in the directions of the document would make the Norembega River the present-day Hudson River, a conclusion which is
not validated by the Ribero image which he used for his map. Dee's
river in that image could be any one of the small streams east of
the Ribero bay. [18]

While the contemporary cartographic evidence suggests that
the territory of Norembega was New England, there are instances

---

[18]Goodwin, loc. cit.; Mood, loc. cit.; Rowse, A. L., The Elizabethans and America
(London: Macmillan, 1959), p. 40.

where the word was applied to areas more southerly or at least
confused with such locations. A modern editor of the elder Hakluyt's "Notes on Colonisation," written as promotion of colonies in
general and Gilbert's schemes in particular, concluded that ". . .
it is obvious that Hakluyt had a colony in lat. 35-40 in mind."[19]
Later Elizabethans sometimes equated Norembega with Virginia.
Two examples of that conception are found in John Gerard's Herball
of 1597. Gerard wrote of his source of potato specimens, ". . . I
have received rootes hereof from Virginia, otherwise called Norembega . . . ," and ". . . in the countries of Norembega, and now
called Virginia by the Honourable sir Walter Raleigh. . . ."[20] A
French account of Drake's return from the West Indies repeated
the association with Virginia, "From San Agustin they went to
Norambega, distant some three hundred and fifty leagues, where
they took away Master Lames. . . ."[21] Mendoza's assertions to
Philip II of Spain that Raleigh planned to go to Norembega might
have their origin in the Elizabethan synonymous use of the two
place names or in his belief that Raleigh was to follow exactly in
Gilbert's tracks.[22]

Since the English applied Virginia to most of the eastern
North America coast north of Florida after it became a fashionable
term, it is credible that they were patterning its application as
the earlier Norembega had been used. Such a pattern of usage
weakens the case that Gilbert's colony was to have been in New
England, but it does not totally preclude it. The widespread agreement on cartographic placement of Norembega in the northeast
rather than spreading it along the entire coast north of Florida
together with the Fernandez-Walker data are strong and valid evidence to conclude that Gilbert's Norembega was the New England
coast. As Smith wrote, "Now this part of America New England
hath formerly beene called Norumbega . . . ," and in a marginal

---

[19] Taylor, Original Writings, Vol. I, p. 119; later Miss Taylor concurred that Norembega was the objective. See Taylor, E. G. R., "Instructions to a Colonial Surveyor in
1582," Mariner's Mirror, XXXVII (1951), 57.

[20] Quinn, Roanoke Voyages, Vol. I, pp. 347, 446.

[21] Ibid., Vol. I, p. 310.

[22] Ibid., Vol. II, pp. 719, 728-29, 731.

note, "My first voyage to Norumbega now called New England."[23]

Sources of the Image

Elizabethan promoters of overseas adventure usually began
the history of England's title to North American lands with the
Cabot voyages made in the reign of Henry VII. But among the
Cabot documents available to a Peckham or a Hakluyt, there was
nothing of substantive information which would have been helpful to
backers of Gilbert's schemes.[24] Late Tudor interest in the Cabot
voyages was essentially legal in order to establish a claim to
America which on the one hand was as valid as the Spanish title
based on the Columbian discoveries and on the other for the northeastern coast older than the French claims derived from Verazzano
or Cartier. As the Elizabethans focused more and more on the
mid-latitude sectors of the North American coast, one suspects
that Tudor stress on the Cabot achievement was aimed more at
invalidating French title than Spanish pretention which was handled
by the argument that England was free to explore any new found
land not possessed by a Christian sovereign.

The earliest known English expedition to the North American
coast which might have been a source of substantive knowledge
about the area useful to Gilbert's group was the Rut voyage of
1527. Two ships, the Sampson and the Mary of Guildford, com-
prised the expedition which left Plymouth on July 10, 1527.[25] One
of the ships, after reaching Newfoundland, sailed south along the
coast of Arambec, a word which is assumed to be a variant spelling of Norembega, possibly in search of the strait or isthmus

---

[23] Arber, E. (ed.), Travels and Works of Captain John Smith (Edinburgh: John Grant,
1910), Vol. II, pp. 636, 936. For other associations of Norembega with New England contemporary to Smith, see Gorges, Ferdinando, America Painted to the Life (London: Nath.
Brook, 1658-59), p. 16, and Thwaites, R. G. (ed.), The Jesuit Relations and Allied Documents (New York: Pageant Book Company, 1959), Vol. II, p. 249.

[24] See Hakluyt, Richard, The Principall Navigations Voiages and Discoveries of the
English Nation (Cambridge: University Press, 1965 [facsimile of 1589 edition]), Vol. II,
pp. 509-16, for the limited Cabot materials available in late Tudor times.

[25] Hakluyt, Principall Navigations . . . (facsimile 1589), Vol. II, p. 517; Innes, H. A.,
The Cod Fisheries (New Haven: Yale University Press, 1940), pp. 12-13; Purchas, S.,
Hakluytus Posthumus or Purchas His Pilgrimes (New York: AMS Press, 1965), Vol. XIV,
pp. 304-5.

reported by Verazzano.[26] The voyage extended the entire length
of the coast, along which landings were made and men put ashore.[27]
Other than a letter written from Newfoundland before the southward
coasting and hence devoid of any datum about the New England
coast, Hakluyt had nothing to publish from the voyage. A map
drawn by a canon of St. Paul's who was on the cruise was mentioned but is lost.[28] It is possible, but not proved, that information from the voyage might have been available in Gilbert's time.

The Rut letter described the active international fishery
which he found on his arrival at Newfoundland.[29] While that information was not immediate to Norembega, it did foretell the importance that exploitation of fisheries was to play in later English
development of New England. Men adventuresome enough to cross
the stormy North Atlantic in small fishing vessels probably searched
out new fishing areas and so extended their activities into New
England waters and onto its shores.[30] But by whom and when New
England was included within the sphere of those fishermen remain
matters of conjecture, not evidence. Acts of Parliament attempt-
ing to regulate fishermen's activities attested to English official
awareness, but what information about New England which might

---

[26] For the link with Verazzano see Taylor, E. G. R., Tudor Geography 1485-1583
(New York: Octagon Books, 1968 [reprint of 1930 edition]), p. 11. Ganong discussed the
possibility that Arambec was Norembega in "The Origin of the Place-Names Acadia and
Norumbega," Transactions of the Royal Society of Canada, Third Series, Vol. XI (1917),
Section 2, 111. Other interpretations of the voyage include Biddle, Richard, Memoir
of Sebastian Cabot (Philadelphia: Carey and Lea, 1831), pp. 315-16; Forster, J. R., History of the Voyages and Discoveries Made in the North (London: G. G. J. and J. Robinson,
1786), pp. 289-90, 436; and Kohl, J. G., History of the Discovery of Maine (Portland:
Bailey and Noyes, 1869), in "Documentary History of the State of Maine," Collections of
the Maine Historical Society, Second Series, Vol. I, pp. 283-89.

[27] Biggar, H. P. (ed.), The Precursors of Jacques Cartier 1497-1534, Vol. V of Publications of the Canadian Archives (Ottawa: Government Printing Bureau, 1911), p. 167;
Hakluyt, Principall Navigations . . . (facsimile 1589), Vol. II, p. 517; Locke, John, History of Navigation which appeared as Appendix B in Clarke, J. S., The Progress of Maritime Discovery (London: T. Cadell and W. Davies, 1803), Vol. I, p. 133; and Hoffman,
B. G., Cabot to Cartier (Toronto: University of Toronto Press, 1961), pp. 117-21.

[28] Kohl, J. G., Descriptive Catalogue of Those Maps, Charts and Surveys Relating to
America (Washington: Henry Polkinhorn, 1857), pp. 24-25.

[29] Purchas, op. cit., Vol. XIV, pp. 304-5.

[30] On such a supposition rests the claim that Europeans preceded Verazzano to the
Maine coast.

have originated among fishermen always reluctant to share their fortunate secrets is another unknown point. One must settle for the probability that some knowledge of those activities filtered beyond the fishers' community into the body of data available to Gilbert and his associates, and that the references in the litera- ture of his schemes to exploitation of fishing reflected the associ- ates' knowledge of northwestern Atlantic fisheries.[31]

Between Rut's return and Gilbert's time materials descriptive of the geography of Norembega available to planners of a colony there were meager, their sparsity reflecting the general English lack of concern for the New World during that period, excepting perhaps their participation in the Newfoundland fishery. Hore's voyage of 1536 might be in the latter category, but the report from it offered no data on Norembega.[32] During the interval Barlow's revised version of a Spanish geography, originally written in 1518, was presented to Henry VIII about 1540. The revised text made no mention of Norembega but described Newfoundland as devoid of spices, gems, and precious metals which would be found only in the tropics where Barlow suggested the English seek them.[33] Eden's translation of Peter Martyr's Decades, a more knowledgeable and precise source than Barlow, also contained nothing of Norembega, except for brief references to Cabot, Gomez, and Cartier, about whom more extensive information might have been available else- where.[34] Those two excursions into Spanish writings on the New World should have convinced the English that the Spanish knew lit- tle about and had little contact with the latitudes of Norembega.

In sum, to obtain information about the mid-latitude coast of eastern North America Gilbert and his associates had to rely more on the limited experience of their contemporaries than of their

---

[31] Quinn, Voyages and Colonising Enterprises, Vol. II, pp. 315, 406, 465-66.

[32] Hakluyt, Principal Navigations . . . (1904), Vol. VIII, pp. 3-7; Hakluyt, Principall Navigations . . . (facsimile 1589), Vol. II, pp. 517-19; Kohl, History of the Discovery, pp. 337-40; and Hoffman, op. cit., pp. 187-88.

[33] Barlow, Roger, A Brief Summe of Geographie (London: Hakluyt Society, 1932), p. 179.

[34] Arber, E. (ed.), The First Three English Books on America (Birmingham: n.p., 1885); and Taylor, Tudor Geography, pp. 19-23.

predecessors. To fill part of the data void they sponsored their own reconnaissance of the coast by sending the Portuguese pilot Fernandez in 1579 and John Walker in 1580 to the coast of Norembega.[35] David Ingram was summoned to relate his experiences. Ingram had been a member of Hawkins' ill-fated West Indian venture. Having been shipwrecked somewhere along the coast of the Gulf of Mexico, he and two other survivors walked northeastward across the continent to the Atlantic where they were eventually rescued. In addition to testifying before a group headed by Sir Francis Walsingham, Ingram was also examined by Doctor Dee whom the associates consulted regularly on matters pertaining to the proposed colony.[36] The narrative of Ingram's stroll contained many fanciful items and some lapses from truth pardonable because of the decade interval between his experience and his testimony, but he also exaggerated and embellished to please his listeners. Since they had no basis for comparison, his embellishments did not impair his relationship with them, for he was one of the few Englishmen then known to have been in Norembega.[37]

If the associates had searched into contemporaneous Spanish or Portuguese materials from the New World, the conclusion on the value of those items reached in the evaluation of the earlier Barlow and Eden translations was reaffirmed. However much they kindled interest and hope of fabled riches, they contained little on the character of the mid-latitude coast about which the English sought information. The Spanish public record for the area began and ended with Gomez. Except for passages such as Santa Cruz' _Islario_ describing the Gamas river, which would have provided a comparison for the Walker report, Iberian writers had only the date of the Gomez voyage, its failure to find the Northwest Passage and ridiculous return, and confusion on the direction of his cruise to relate.[38]

---

[35]_Calendar of State Papers_, op. cit., p. 2; De Costa, loc. cit.; McCann, F. T., _English Discovery of America to 1585_ (New York: King's Crown Press of Columbia University, 1952), p. 159; Read, op. cit., Vol. III, p. 399; and Taylor, _Tudor Geography_, p. 125.

[36]Halliwell, op. cit., p. 17.

[37]_Calendar of State Papers_, op. cit., p. 2; De Costa, op. cit., pp. 6-7; Hakluyt, _Principall Navigations_ . . . (facsimile 1589), Vol. II, pp. 557-62. Hakluyt deleted Ingram's narrative from the second (1599-1600) edition of _Principall Navigations_.

[38]In addition to Santa Cruz other Iberian authors whose works were available were

If Walsingham's agents were able to penetrate into official secrets, nothing is known to have come from that source. To compilers of New World data such as Hakluyt, Iberian materials must have been profoundly disappointing by their lack of information north of Florida. A prominent biographer of the younger Hakluyt asserted that after Gilbert's failure he went to Paris to continue his collection of data because as a Protestant chaplain he would not have been allowed to enter Spain in a diplomatic capacity.[39] A more important consideration which the biographer realized was that the Spanish had already proved to be limited sources, while the French had been otherwise. Not political or religious considerations sent Hakluyt to Paris; the availability of relevant materials led him there.

The French provided not only a larger body of knowledge about the mid-latitude eastern coast of North America but also a continuity of experience lacking to both the English and Spanish. English awareness of that circumstance was indicated by Hakluyt's use of French materials and, here hypothesized, by the Elizabethan stress on Cabot's discovery and the placement of their interests south of a New France delimited around the River of Canada.[40] Besides the brief Verazzano material, the Cartier reports were singularly important because of their detailed information and the fact that they described an area close enough to the latitudes of Norembega to provide some comparative conjectures. Significantly they were translated into English about the time that Gilbert's preparations were being made.[41] Of Cartier's immediate successors Alfonse provided the earliest first hand information about Norembega.[42]

Gomara, Galvano, Martyr, and Oviedo. See Chapter I, footnote 23.

[39] Parks, G. B., Richard Hakluyt and the English Voyages (New York: American Geographical Society, 1928), pp. 99-100.

[40] Note the inclusion of Verazzano and Cartier materials in Divers Voyages and Principall Navigations. Additional French influence may perhaps be seen in Peckham's Catholic colony idea having its origin in the concept of a New France as a refuge for French Huguenots.

[41] Yates, op. cit., pp. 55-56; Hakluyt, Principal Navigations . . . (1904), Vol. VIII, pp. 183-274, for Cartier selections, pp. 283-99 for Roberval material.

[42] Biggar, H. P., The Early Trading Companies of New France (Toronto: University of Toronto Library, 1901), p. 31; Hoffman, op. cit., pp. 168-71, 230-31; Ganong, W. F.,

He was reputedly followed there by André Thevet, one of whose books had preceded Cartier into an English translation.[43] From Ramusio was the relation of a Dieppe captain, Pierre Crignon, who probably visited the coast in the late 1520's or early 1530's.[44] Like Crignon and other unknown French seamen, the activities of men like Stephen Bellenger on the Norembega coast may have been more frequent in practice than occurrence in surviving documents. Bellenger was a Norman merchant, following in the tracks of Cartier, Alfonse, and Crignon--to list only the known--who was involved in the fur trade.[45] France, not Spain, was the obvious fruitful source of Norembega data.

The Image

A critical component of the Elizabethan image of Norembega was the character of the settlement which Gilbert and his associates hoped to establish there. Their image included a future fiefdom, a feudal model of England transplanted across the Atlantic. The immediate plans and functions of the colony, however, are among the mysteries of the whole venture. Because the ships did not carry families, livestock, or agricultural implements, we may assume that initially the colony was to prepare for future arrivals and was not expected to be, indeed could not be, self-sustaining. If arrangements were made to supply the colony with necessities from England, no record of such plans survived. Perhaps supplying was contingent upon return to England of some word of the planting of the colony and its location. Gilbert and his associates in their failure to comprehend that a colony so distant from home could not survive or flourish exclusively on imported necessities

---

Crucial Maps in the Early Cartography and Place-Nomenclature of the Atlantic Coast of Canada (Toronto: University of Toronto Press, 1964), pp. 364-84; and Hakluyt, Principal Navigations . . . (1904), Vol. VIII, pp. 275-83.

[43]Thevet, André, The New Found Worlde or Antarctike (London: T. Hacket for Henrie Bynneman, 1568).

[44]Hoffman, op. cit., pp. 169-70.

[45]Taylor, Original Writings, Vol. I, pp. 205-6, Vol. II, pp. 227, 266-67; Quinn, D. B., "The Voyage of Etienne Bellenger to the Maritimes in 1583: A New Document," Canadian Historical Review, XLIII (1962), 328-43.

were no better and no worse than later developers of Roanoke or
Jamestown. It was a lesson that required many failures and deaths
before it was learned by English adventurers.

The long range vision of the colony may be abstracted from
Gilbert's will and his agreements with his associates.[46] The
Queen's patent gave Gilbert feudal rights over the land which he
was to appropriate. To finance the scheme he assigned some of
those rights together with land to men willing to back the enterprise. The land was to be settled by families, productive farms
and manufactures to be developed, towns, villages, and transportation to be established as well as exploitation of raw materials
needed and saleable in England. He willed to his wife and sons the
revenues to be levied on those activities in the lands directly settled by him. Comparable developments were envisioned to occur in
the associates' lands, on which feudal taxes were to be collected
as vassal payments to Gilbert or his heirs. A gigantic fiefdom in
the New World had been designed and was to be realized by an im-
mense transplanting of Elizabethan political, social, and economic
institutions and English land and settlement patterns.[47]

The concept of a resident, self-sustaining population meant
that consideration of Norembega's agricultural potentialities was a
consistent theme about which information was sought. The Gomez
legends on the various editions of the Ribero maps contained brief
but specifically favorable statements on the productivity of the
area.[48] From the same period was the testimony of Verazzano who
made assessments at various places along the coast. At one of his
landings he found conditions suitable for grape growing and named
the place "Arcadia" because of the beauty and bounty of its trees.
Refugio was also pronounced arable because of the practice of agriculture there by the natives, but his northernmost landing he con-

---

[46] Slafter, op. cit., pp. 288-89.

[47] An additional function of the colony might have been as a base of operations against
the Spanish West Indies. If that function had a high priority among the sponsors, secrecy
was judicious for its effectiveness as well as diplomatic politeness. But because of the
elaborate design of the Gilbert will and his agreements with the associates, it is untenable
to assume that a naval station was the sole motive of the Gilbert expedition.

[48] See Chapter I, p. 20.

sidered as sterile and uninviting as the natives were nasty. He deemed the area useful only for its trees.[49] In the writings of Cartier were descriptions of native agriculture conducted north and west of Norembega, evidence that the northern areas were arable.[50] Later Alfonse attested to the practice of agriculture in Norembega.[51] Crignon depicted Norembega as a land whose soil yielded abundant fruit, although some too exotic, i. e. oranges and almonds, to have been seen there.[52] Thevet gave a general promise of the rich potentiality of American agriculture. However, for the latitudes closest to Norembega about which he made specific statements, he listed some characteristics such as hailstorms, earthquakes, and extreme cold which were not encouraging for agriculture,[53] but he was the minority opinion. In their own time, Gilbert's group obtained reassurance that agriculture was practicable in Norembega. Ingram included fertile and fruitful soils among the characteristics which he detailed from his journey.[54] Walker in 1580 returned from the River of Norembega to report that "the Country was most excellent both for the soyle, diuersity of sweete woode and other trees."[55] Direct references to the soil and indirect ones based on vegetation agreed that Norembega was suitable for English crops.

Of the climate of Norembega the sources were surprisingly silent, perhaps because none of the observers stayed long enough to obtain data. Hints of unfavorable conditions such as storms and

---

[49]Bacchiani, Alessandro, "Giovanni da Verazzano and his Discoveries in North America 1524, " Annual Report of the American Scenic and Historic Preservation Society, XV (1910), 186-87, 194, 196-97; and Hakluyt, Principal Navigations . . . (1904), Vol. VIII, pp. 429-30, 436-37.

[50]Hakluyt, Principal Navigations . . . (1904), Vol. VIII, pp. 232-33, 241.

[51]Ibid., Vol. VIII, p. 282.   [52]Hoffman, op. cit., p. 170.

[53]Thevet, op. cit., pp. 122, 132-33. Thevet's visit to Norembega was described only in his Cosmographie of 1575 where the materials appear to be borrowed from Cartier or otherwise spurious. Whether or not the Elizabethans recognized the invalidity of Thevet's writings is not known. See Hoffman, op. cit., pp. 178-79; and Parks, op. cit., pp. 114, 119.

[54]Hakluyt, Principall Navigations . . . (facsimile 1589), Vol. II, p. 559; and De Costa, op. cit., p. 6.

[55]De Costa, op. cit., p. 7.

cold weather did not prompt any systematic assessment.[56] There
was occasional reassurance that Norembega was less severe than
Newfoundland. "Ffor this coaste Norembega ys never subjecte to
the Ise, wch is never lightly scene to the southe of Cape Razo in
Newfounde lande."[57] The presence of familiar flora was construed
as evidence both that the climate was comparable to England's and
that European crops could be grown. Further support for those
assumptions was the Elizabethan association of climatic characteristics of the New World with those of West European areas on identical parallels.

The early explorers quickly noted that the vegetation of eastern North American coast contained many species known to them
from western Europe as well as exotic flora which they could not
recognize. It has been observed that nowhere else could they have
gone so far across the sea and found so much so familiar to them.[58]
While that coincidence led them into some unfortunate conclusions
about the climate, it also facilitated their use of the forests.
Verazzano would have been the earliest source of information about
the vegetation. His most detailed description of New World flora
was Arcadia, a land south of the latitudes of Norembega according
to the text of the Roman letter but variously placed on maps of the
era, where the luxuriant and park-like forests were seen. The offshore island near Refugio was "covered with trees" which the
natives were burning.[59] At Refugio the forest had been removed
by field clearing for a considerable distance around the native villages. He described the remaining forest, "entering then into the
woods, all of which are penetrable by any numerous army in any
way whatsoever, and whose trees, oaks, cypresses, and others,
are unknown in our Europe. We found Lucallian apples, plums and
filberts, and many kinds of fruits different from ours."[60] His
landfall in Maine was at ". . . a high land full of very thick forests,

---

[56]Thevet, op. cit., pp. 122, 132-33; Hakluyt, Principall Navigations . . . (facsimile
1589), Vol. II, p. 550.

[57]Taylor, Original Writings, Vol. II, p. 267.

[58]Sauer, Carl O., "The Settlement of the Humid East," Climate and Man: Yearbook
of Agriculture (Washington: Government Printing Office, 1941), 159.

[59]Bacchiani, op. cit., p. 189.   [60]Ibid., p. 193.

the trees of which were pines, cypresses and such as grow in cold regions. "[61]

Later sources added little to those brief remarks from Verazzano. In one instance, that of Crignon, subtropical fruit trees were inaccurately placed in Norembega.[62] Most reports reiterated the vast forests and mentioned ". . . dyvers kinds of fruits and trees of great eastimatione."[63] Walker's "sweete woods" was a typically terse description.[64] Ingram's testimony contained the pattern of almost equal stress on the exotic and familiar "like ours in England."[65]

Ingram's narrative likewise had many references to animal life, in which the exotic equalled the familiar. He talked of strange beasts and "birds of all sortes as we have, and many strange birds." He claimed to have seen bears, wolves, lynx, foxes, deer, and hares, all familiar to his listeners and readers, but his assertion that "cattel like ours" existed there must be considered a fable.[66] He described the American bison as ". . . a kinde of beast almost as bigge agayne as an oxe in the shape of body not much differinge from an oxe, savinge that he hath eares of a great bigness, that are in fashione much like unto the eares of a bloodhound havinge thereon very long heare, and lykewise on his breast, and other parts of his bodye long heare."[67]

Probably more important to his examiners than the enumeration of species was the economic significance of the rich and abundant furs.[68] Tangible evidence for them was the cargo of buffalo hides brought back by Walker and the pelts obtained by the French.[69] The prospect of immediate revenue from marketable furs was a factor to promote investment in the colonial scheme.

---

[61] Ibid., p. 196.

[62] Hoffman, op. cit., p. 170.

[63] De Costa, op. cit., p. 7.

[64] Ibid.

[65] Hakluyt, Principall Navigations . . . (facsimile 1589), Vol. II, p. 560.

[66] Ibid.

[67] De Costa, op. cit., p. 6.

[68] Ibid., pp. 6-7.

[69] Quinn, Voyages and Colonising Enterprises, Vol. I, p. 50, and "The Voyage of Etienne Bellenger . . . ," loc. cit.; Biggar, Early Trading Companies, p. 31.

Every part of the New World was hoped to contain precious metals and gems. Although the Elizabethans had been embarrassed by the furor over Frobisher's fraudulent ore, the image of Norembega held modest promise as a source of riches. Ingram probably played to the obvious, if then restrained, cupidity of the times when "he confessed that there is a great aboundance of gold, silver and pearle and that he hath seanne at the heads of dyvers springs and in smale rounninge brouks dyvers peaces of gold soume as bigge as his fynger, others as bigge as his fyst and peaces of dyvers bignes."[70] But his statement that the French captain who rescued him near Cape Breton had traded trivia to the natives for ruby and wrought silver is difficult for the modern reader to accept.[71] Walker reported in 1580 that a silver mine was found near the River of Norembega, although no one has been able to locate it since.[72]

Of other minerals only iron and salt received passing mention from Ingram, and they did not loom importantly, although the mercantilistic argument of colonies to supply needed raw materials was already circulating in England.[73] The presence of iron ore was attractive to those who hoped to augment English production by import from colonial areas.[74] Marsh salt was linked to future development of fisheries.[75]

Norembega held the possibility of controlling the Atlantic entrance to a northwest passage. Lok, for example, believed in the existence of the Verazzano isthmus and sea and on his map placed Norembega just north of the narrow neck.[76] Other evidence

---

[70]De Costa, op. cit., p. 6.

[71]Hakluyt, Principall Navigations . . . (facsimile 1589), Vol. II, p. 561.

[72]De Costa, op. cit., p. 7; Calendar of State Papers, op. cit., p. 2.

[73]See the elder Hakluyt's "Notes on Colonisation (1578)" in Taylor, Original Writings, Vol. I, pp. 119ff.

[74]Mc Manis, Douglas R., "English Evaluation of North American Iron during the Late Sixteenth and Early Seventeenth Centuries," Professional Geographer, XXI (March, 1969), 93-96.

[75]Hakluyt, Principall Navigations . . . (facsimile 1589), Vol. II, p. 559.

[76]See reproduction of the Lok map in Hakluyt, Principal Navigations . . . (1904), Vol. VII, p. 368.

supported the idea that the River of Norembega might be a strait
connecting the Atlantic to the western ocean or northern sea whose
nearness had been related by Indians to Cartier and which Ingram
claimed to have seen. [77] With an outpost at such a location England
could both harrass and rival Spain and Portugal. [78]

As everything else which the Elizabethans could learn of
Norembega, their knowledge of the natives was sketchy and a composite of information drawn from a larger area than Norembega
itself. Verazzano found the northern Indians hostile, uncoopera-
tive, and brutish. They wore skins of "bears, lynes, and sea-
wolves, " and had copper pieces in their ears. They did not practice
agriculture but lived by a hunting-gathering-fishing economy. [79] In
contrast he depicted the natives of Refugio in terms which suggest
Rousseau's noble savage, ". . . the most beautiful people and the
most civilized in customs that we have found in this navigation, "
friendly, and generous. [80] Materially they were like the northern
Indians in the use of skins for dress and copper for body orna-
ments. They dwelt in wigwams made of sapling frames covered
with mats which were removed and taken when their villages were
transferred to new sites. [81] Around their villages were large
expanses of cultivated fields. However objective Verazzano's
descriptions seem to a modern reader, they must have disappointed
Elizabethans to the extent that they were devoid of any suggestion
that Norembega's natives were comparable to the Aztecs or Incas.

Ingram's description of the Indians was characteristically
more fabulous than was Verazzano's. He related,

---

[77] Hakluyt, Principal Navigations . . . (1904), Vol. VIII, pp. 245-46; Hakluyt, Principall Navigations . . . (facsimile 1589), Vol. II, p. 562; Biggar, H. P. (ed.), A Collection of Documents Relating to Jacques Cartier and the Sieur de Roberval, Vol. XIV of
Publications of the Public Archives of Canada (Ottawa: Public Archives of Canada, 1930),
p. 771.

[78] Taylor, Original Writings, Vol. II, pp. 240, 315, 317.

[79] Bacchiani, op. cit., p. 196. Verazzano was the first European to record the significant cultural divide--agricultural versus non-agricultural--between the Indians of
northern and southern New England.

[80] Ibid., p. 190.

[81] Ibid., p. 193. Here Verazzano recognized the semi-sedentary habits of the
Eastern Woodland Indians.

ffurther yt the men goe naked savinge only the mydell part of them covered with skynnes of beasts and wth leaves, And that generallye all men weare about there armes dyvers hoopes of gold and silver wch are of good thicknes and lykewyse they weare the lyke about the smale of there leggs wch hoopes are garnished wth pearle dyvers of them as bigge as ones thume.

That the womenne of the countrye gooe apareled wth plats of gold over there body much lyke unto an armor about the middest of there bodye they weare leafes, wch hath growinge there one very longe much lyke unto heare. and lykwyse about there armes and the smale of there leggs they weare hoopes of gold and sylver garnyshed wth fayer pearle.[82]

Although he presented an accurate description of the shapes of the native houses, he distorted the interiors with massive crystal pillars covered with gold and silver objects. Fernandez and Walker repeated the shape of the dwellings but did not decorate them with precious metals.[83] Hence the last reports before Gilbert's sailing were the eye-witness accounts of sensible Elizabethan seamen, not the confused Ingram.

Except for Verazzano's portrait of the hostile natives who tried to prevent his landing, the natives appeared primitive, peaceful, and docile enough that they could not effectively stop an English invasion of their lands. As non-Christians they were subject to the terms of the Queen's patent which empowered Gilbert to claim any non-Christian territory regardless of indigenous occupancy.[84]

The Elizabethan image of Norembega was incomplete in spite of the purposive efforts to obtain valid data about the region. Little direct information was available. Some of it was correct, but much of it was confused, imprecise, inaccurate, or fanciful. Gilbert's attempt to colonize such a vaguely known region was burdened not only by an image unsatisfactory to make adequate preparations but also by his own shortcomings of personality and leadership. Hayes appropriately summarized the enterprise as much money and men wasted on an "imagined good."[85]

---

[82]De Costa, op. cit., p. 6.   [83]Ibid., p. 7.

[84]Hakluyt, Principall Navigations . . . (facsimile 1589), Vol. II, pp. 677-79.

[85]Quinn, Voyages and Colonising Enterprises, Vol. II, p. 422. Interest, however, did not dissolve immediately. Carlisle, stepson of Walsingham, flirted briefly with a plan to continue Gilbert's colonization scheme in Norembega, but the plan came to naught. See Calendar of State Papers, op. cit., p. 1.

CHAPTER III

FRENCH REJECTION OF THE COAST

French and English explorers arrived on the New England coast almost simultaneously at the beginning of the 1600's. Legal conflict between the two countries over title to the coast began in the reign of Elizabeth I when the English boasted the discovery of the Cabots to supersede the French claims based on the Verazzano voyage. But with agents of each country along the coast the situation moved closer to the outbreak of imperial conflicts which would continue intermittently for a century and a half until the defeated French were forced from the continent. Long before that culmination the French surveyed the New England coast and rejected it as the focus of their activities. As a result French interest in New England was peripheral to their concern for Canada and limited to forays into English occupied areas and efforts to define an advantageous Maine-Acadia border.

French activities on the coast in the first decades of the 1600's fell into two phases. The first involved the evaluation of the coast as a locale for a permanent fur collection station. It lasted less than five years, and during it Champlain made his first important contributions as an American explorer. The second phase, even briefer, was an abortive Jesuit mission to the Maine Indians.

French fur traders had been active along the New England coast at least as early as the last two decades of the sixteenth century, perhaps even earlier.[1] The French government made North

---

[1] See Biggar, H. P., The Early Trading Companies of New France (Toronto: University of Toronto Library, 1901); Bishop, Morris, Champlain: The Life of Fortitude (New York: Alfred A. Knopf, 1948), p. 33; Innes, H. A., The Fur Trade in Canada (New Haven: Yale University Press, 1930), pp. 5-19; and Quinn, D. B., "The Voyage of Etienne Bellenger to the Maritimes in 1583: A New Document," Canadian Historical Review, XLIII (1962), 328-43, for studies of French fur trade activities before 1600.

American fur trade an item of official policy in 1603 when Henry IV of France granted a monopoly of the coast's fur trade to Sieur de Monts for ten years.[2] Because of opposition from other French interests who were excluded by the terms of the monopoly, the grant was revoked. But the king's grant was an official direct challenge to English interests then probing the coast.

Initially rejecting a location on either the Bay of Fundy or Nova Scotia's south coast for his post, de Monts sent three expeditions southward to find a satisfactory base of operations. Champlain participated in each of them, and his journals and maps are the earliest sources of comprehensive and detailed information of the area.[3]

The first exploration of the coast began in early summer, 1604, when a party left the temporary camp at Port Royal and sailed around the Bay of Fundy to the mouth of the St. John River where the Frenchmen had their first view of wild North American grapes. From there the group went to the islands at the entrance of Passamaquoddy Bay. Because of the large flocks of magpies observed there, the French called those islands the Magpie Islands. On them and nearby Grand Manan were seen "several good harbors for vessels."[4] On the trip from the Magpie Islands through the bay into the River of the Etechemins, as the French styled the St. Croix River, more islands, too numerous to be counted and of various size, were passed. Again the existence of many harbors on them was recorded. That feature, together with the presence of abundant cod, salmon, bass, herring, and halibut, made the area a satisfactory place for fishermen, which the de Monts' group was not.

---

[2] Bishop, op. cit., p. 58; Calendar of State Papers, Colonial Series (London: H. M. Stationery Office, 1860), Vol. I, p. 4.

[3] See Chapter I of this study for discussion of his maps.

[4] Translated versions of Champlain's reports appear in Champlain's Voyages (Boston: Prince Society, 1878-82), 3 vols., and Biggar, H. P. (ed.), The Works of Samuel de Champlain (Toronto: Champlain Society, 1922-36), 6 vols. The text relative to New England has been reprinted in Levermore, C. H. (ed.), Forerunners and Competitors of the Pilgrims and Puritans (Brooklyn: New England Society of Brooklyn, 1912), Vol. I, pp. 69-170. Page citations here are to the Prince Society edition. Champlain's Voyages, Vol. II, p. 31.

Passing up the river a short distance, the French party encountered two islands, the larger of which was surrounded by short rocky cliffs except for one sandy point. It was some "nine hundred to a thousand paces" from the shore, a situation which would permit cannon to control the river. The French were aware of the dangers to which they were exposed by settling among potentially hostile natives, who on the other hand were necessary to the commerce which the French planned to develop and whom they hoped to convert to Christianity. The island had good soil and was covered with firs, birch, maples, and oaks. Its clayey soil was considered usable for "making brick and other . . . articles."[5]

Upstream where a falls stopped navigation, the French found a clearing of fifteen to twenty acres where they sowed wheat which was later reported to have ripened. The dense forests were thought to be the only barrier to making the area productive of grain. The French were told that the headwaters of the stream were only a short portage from the rivers of St. John and Norembega.[6]

The larger island, which Champlain described as well situated and well provided, was chosen the most suitable site for de Monts' post and named St. Croix Island. During the construction of buildings mosquitoes were a constant plague to the workers, one of the few mentions of insect pests which Champlain provided.[7] Ultimately the post had a storehouse, houses for the men, and a cannonade (Figure 14).[8]

With experience the island proved to be less than a desirable habitat. Attempts to grow crops failed. Seeds germinated well, but once above ground the sprouts quickly withered and died in the

---

[5] Ibid., Vol. II, pp. 31-32.

[6] Ibid., Vol. II, pp. 33-34. Lescarbot said that the grain was oats, a more probable choice to do well in that climate. The text of Lescarbot's Histoire de la Nouvelle France (1609) as translated into English in 1609 was reprinted by Purchas in his collection and in Levermore, op. cit., Vol. I, pp. 171-307. Page citations for Lescarbot in this study are to the annotated Levermore version. See Levermore, op. cit., Vol. I, p. 192.

[7] The island is now called de Monts' Island in honor of the French leader. Champlain's Voyages, Vol. II, pp. 34-35.

[8] Levermore, op. cit., Vol. I, p. 197; Shurtleff, H. R., The Log Cabin Myth (Cambridge: Harvard University Press, 1939), pp. 66-67.

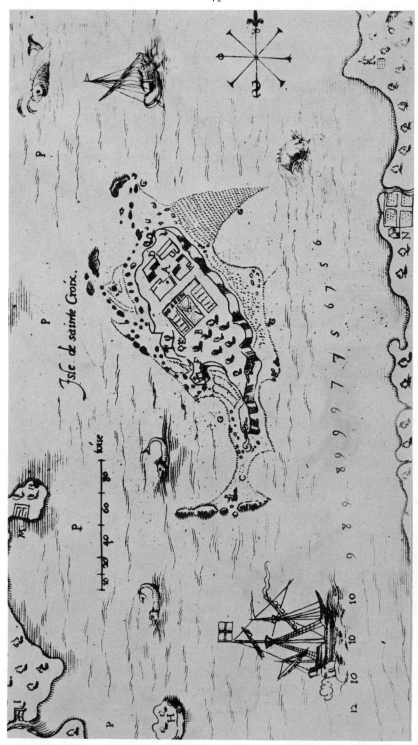

Fig. 14. --Champlain's Sketch of the French Post on St. Croix Island

hot sun and dry sandy soil. Rainfall was inadequate to sustain the plants, for it evidently was one of the dry summers which periodically occur throughout the Northeast.[9] The lack of water extended to human needs, but Champlain was silent on that shortcoming. It was left to Lescarbot to remind his countrymen that "an island without streams of fresh water for drinking and housekeeping is not a fit place for the establishment of a colony; and these small islands have none." During the winter the colonists were beset by a shortage of fire wood because the island's timber had been consumed in construction of buildings.[10]

While Lescarbot did not disavow Champlain's and others' optimistic assessment of the general area of the St. Croix, he did question that the site achieved security which in the final analysis was the dominant criterion for de Monts' choice.[11] Lescarbot thought that the island was too isolated from incoming Frenchmen. ". . . It is meete to tell you how hard the Ile of St. Croix is to bee found out, to them that were never there. For there are so many Iles and great Bayes to goe by, before one be at it, that I wonder how ever one might pierce so farre for to finde it."[12] Agreeing that the colonists should protect themselves from possible hostilities of the natives, he argued that the island, devoid of water and timber and with its gardens on the mainland, was not a location to realize optimum security from attack. ". . . If at any time, morning, noon and night it is necessary to cross (and with great difficulty) a large body of water, to obtain from the mainland every necessity. Suppose there should be danger from an enemy; how should workmen protect themselves, if isolated on the mainland, engaged in some necessary labor and suddenly pursued? Boats could not always be at their call at any given point nor two men to row them."

Lescarbot ascribed the lamentable toll of disease and death which occurred at the post during the winter to the northern exposure of the fort. "But above all must there be protection from the

---

[9] Champlain's Voyages, Vol. II, p. 50.

[10] Levermore, op. cit., Vol. I, pp. 185, 198.

[11] Bishop, op. cit., p. 66.   [12] Levermore, op. cit., Vol. I, p. 191.

rude winds and the cold, which protection it is impossible to have
in a small space surrounded by water. "[13] He thought that bad
waters and unhealthy north winds caused the scurvy which was diag-
nosed as the trouble. "But there is yet in New France another bad
qualitie of the aire, by reason of Lakes that be thicke there, and
of the great rottennesse in the woods, whose odour the bodies having drawne up, during the raines of Autumne and Winter, easily
are ingendred the corruptions of the mouth, and swelling in the
legges before spoken, and a cold entreth unsensibly into it which
benummeth the limbs. . . ."[14]

Champlain reported that the winter began earlier than expected and that it was more severe and longer than those of France.
Nothing in their French experience prepared them for the severe
continental type winters which are characteristic of these latitudes
in eastern North America. The snowfall during that first winter
for resident Europeans in a Maine winter was heavy and still three
to four feet deep at the end of April. Lescarbot noted that the winter varied in intensity from year to year and speculated on the
cause.[15]

> But I am not yet fully satisfied in searching the cause, why in one and the selfesame
> parallel the season is in those parts of New France more slow by a moneth than in
> these parts, and the leaves appeare not upon the trees but towards the end of the
> moneth of May: unless wee say that the thicknesse of the wood and the greatnesse of
> the Forrests doe hinder the Sunne from warming the ground: Item, that the Country
> where we were is joyning to the Sea, and thereby more subject to cold . . . and
> besides that, the land having never beene tilled is the more dampish, the trees and
> plants not being able easily to draw sap from their mother the earth.

To Champlain's mind the winter was the cause of the scurvy, for
"those who continued sick were healed by spring, which commences
in this country in May. That led us to believe that the change of
season restored their health rather than the remedies prescribed."
The winter's physical discomfort was increased by the lack of fuel
and water because the men were unable to go to the mainland for
those necessities whenever the river was jammed with ice flows
drifted by the tide. As explanation for the failure to be prepared

---

[13] Ibid., Vol. I, p. 185.

[14] Ibid., Vol. I, p. 203. See pp. 198-206 for Lescarbot's discussion of the causes of
scurvy.

[15] Champlain's Voyages, Vol. II, pp. 49-53; Levermore, op. cit., Vol. I, p. 283.

for the winter, Champlain's apology highlighted the inadequate information based only on summer reconnaissance. "It would be very difficult to ascertain the character of this region without spending a winter in it; for, on arriving here in summer, every thing is very agreeable, in consequence of woods, fine country, and many varieties of good fish which are found there." The lesson was learned; henceforth natives were asked about winter conditions. De Monts' decision to abandon St. Croix Island because of the harsh winter and to seek a site with a milder climate foreboded the later English experience on the Kennebec. [16]

After the island had been selected as the site for the post and during the initial construction, Champlain with a small party continued to survey southward along the coast. The party which left the island on September 2, 1604, included two natives who were to serve as guides and translators. During the sailing the dense fogs which frequently hang over the coast delayed their passage. They were, nevertheless, able to see some of the numerous islands, banks, and rocks of that coast. Champlain considered the trees-- chiefly pine and fir--on the islands to be inferior. Passing too close to one island, a boat was damaged on a submerged rock. That Island he described as ". . . very high and notched in places, so that there is the appearance to one at sea, as of seven or eight mountains extending along near each other. The summit of most of them is destitute of trees, as there are only rocks on them. The woods consist of pines, firs and birches only." The name which Champlain bestowed on the desolate island remains today--Mount Desert Island. The only positive feature of those islands which he stressed was the many fine harbors, and he concluded that they were unsuitable for permanent settlement. [17]

A significant contribution from that voyage occurred when the two guides persuaded a group of natives who were fishing and beaver hunting to lead the French to their settlement which was on the River of Pentegoüet, now the Penobscot. Champlain identified the stream as the River of Norembega. Based on what he saw, he

---

[16] Bishop, op. cit., p. 75; Champlain's Voyages, Vol. II, pp. 52-55. He also stated that the diet of salted meat and vegetables was "partial cause of these dreadful maladies."

[17] Champlain's Voyages, Vol. II, p. 39.

discredited all earlier descriptions of the area. While he conceded that previous explorers might have visited its mouth, he branded the reports of a fabled Norembega as pretense and fraud. [18]

Champlain's description of the Penobscot began with detailed directions of sightings and positions to pick the course through the numerous islands of its mouth into the main channel. A short distance upstream he was forced to anchor his boats first by rocks exposed at low tide and beyond them by a seven to eight feet falls. The surrounding countryside was forested with oaks on one side of the river and on the other pines with a few firs. The absence of any town or village and the lack of evidence of previous settlements perhaps best illustrated the contradiction between the reports which he had read of Norembega and the landscape which he was viewing. He saw no settlement, only one or two empty cabins which were bark covered wigwams comparable to those which he had seen in Nova Scotia. [19] In contrast he had read of a dense population which made cotton yarn. [20] He concluded that the native population was small and that they were Etechemins who wore skins and furs and were otherwise in habits similar to Canadian and Nova Scotian Indians. The Maine tribe was semi-nomadic and in their quest for subsistence practiced a transhumance which brought them to the coast and coastal islands in the summer for game and fish, while during the winter they retreated inland to hunt and moved about wherever and whenever game could be found. [21] With factual accounts circulating in the writings of Champlain and Lescarbot the myths of a fabulous Norembega were laid to rest until they were revived in the late nineteenth century by Americans who linked the myths to the Vikings. [22]

---

[18]Ibid., Vol. II, p. 41; Levermore, op. cit., Vol. I, p. 215. Lescarbot agreed in the censor of the earlier reports of Norembega. He attacked Alfonse's tale in particular. ". . . Of the said Jean Alphonse I credit not at all, except his one statement that the river of which we speak has at its entrance many islands, banks, and rocks." Both critics continued to use the place name on their maps.

[19]Champlain's Voyages, Vol. II, pp. 43-44; Levermore, op. cit., Vol. I, p. 213.

[20]Champlain's Voyages, Vol. II, pp. 40-41.

[21]Ibid., Vol. II, pp. 44-47; Levermore, op. cit., Vol. I, pp. 212, 215.

[22]Mc Manis, Douglas R., "The Traditions of Vinland," Annals of the Association of American Geographers, LIX (December, 1969), 805.

Another important contribution of that first French survey of the New England coast was information about the relationship of Maine streams to the St. Lawrence drainage system. Natives told the French party that the River of Norembega rose in a lake which was only a short portage from the St. Croix River. A small river linked that lake to yet another from which a portage led to a stream which entered the St. Lawrence near Quebec.[23] From that informa- tion the French could conclude that the Maine streams did not give access to any large expanse of the continent as did the St. Lawrence.

After the decision to abandon the post on St. Croix Island, de Monts sent another group southward along the coast in hopes of finding a satisfactory location for his enterprise. The French now fully appreciated the importance of native guides to obtain informa- tion about unknown areas and as on the first trip included two native guides/translators "in hopes of exploring and learning more particularly by their aid what the character of this country was. . . . "[24] Departing on June 18, 1605, the party retraced the ear- lier route as far as the mouth of the Kennebec River. Going up- stream, they were disappointed to find the surrounding countryside rocky and unarable. But they did learn that the Kennebec from its source like the Penobscot was linked by portages to a stream which flowed into the St. Lawrence, the first instance of specific Euro- pean knowledge of that corridor. The natives thereabouts seemed comparable in habits, dress, and subsistence to those near the post and to those whom they had encountered at the Penobscot, but they were the first natives whom the French had contacted with any knowledge of agriculture. They did not practice it because their

---

[23] Champlain's Voyages, Vol. II, p. 47. Champlain's description of this relationship is out of place in his narrative. Instead of being part of his discussion of Norembega, it follows the departure from there and the arrival at the mouth of the Kennebec. In the nar- rative of his second voyage when he entered the Kennebec, he stressed a comparable rela- tionship of that stream with the St. Lawrence River. Lescarbot, however, associated the route only with the Kennebec, not the Penobscot. The stream pattern of the area suggests that both writers were correct to the extent that the St. Lawrence could be reached by por- tage from the headwaters of either river. A connection to the St. Croix as outlined by Champlain could be made only from the Penobscot. Lescarbot erred by assigning the Kennebec relationship which became known during the second voyage to the first trip. See Levermore, op. cit., Vol. I, p. 215.

[24] Champlain's Voyages, Vol. II, p. 55.

enemies would attack at harvest time and carry away the corn so
that they had ceased to plant. In so far as he had seen the lower
portions of the Kennebec, Champlain considered the areas no more
suitable for the post than other sections he had viewed.[25]

Departure from the Kennebec was delayed by fog. Unfortunately the French did not record their opinion of the effect of these
recurring fogs on the proposed commerce, so that we do not know
what role that factor played in their assessment of the coast. Rich-
mond Island made a more favorable impression on the travelers
than had the Kennebec area. The island was ". . . very beautiful
in view of what it produces; for it has fine oaks and nut-trees, the
soil cleared up, and many vineyards bearing beautiful grapes in
their season."[26] The presence of grapes prompted the name Island
of Bacchus.

Enroute to the Saco River the French crossed from one native
cultural area to another, a fact which they preceived when they
saw the natives of the Saco region. The natives were no longer
the Etechemins but spoke Almouchiquois which the guides could not
understand. In contrast to the docile, friendly, and cooperative
characteristics associated with the Etechemins, the new group
earned a reputation as deceitful, treacherous, and thieving.[27]

On landing at Saco Bay the French saw for the first time the
practice of agriculture by the coastal Indians. Planting was done
on the river banks with a wooden spade.[28]

We saw their Indian corn, which they raise in gardens. Planting three or four kernels
in one place, they then heap up about it a quantity of earth with shells of the signoc
. . . then three feet distant they planted as much more, and thus in succession. With
this corn they put in each hill three or four Brazilian beans, which are of different

---

[25]Ibid., Vol. II, p. 61. This is another example of the French observing that the
northern limit of native agriculture was determined by cultural factors rather than physical ones. The other and better known instance was the disappearance of agriculture from
Montreal in the interim between Cartier and Champlain.

[26]Ibid., Vol. II, p. 62.

[27]Levermore, op. cit., Vol. I, pp. 216, 265. Modern scholars of the American
Indians concur in a major cultural division between northern and southern New England
tribes. See Driver, H. E., Indians of North America (Chicago: University of Chicago
Press, 1961), various maps, and Kroeber, A. L., Cultural and Natural Areas of Native
North America (Berkeley: University of California Press, 1939), map 6.

[28]Champlain's Voyages, Vol. II, pp. 64-66.

colors. When they grow up, they interlace with the corn, which reaches to the height of from five to six feet, and they keep the ground very free from weeds. We saw there many squashes, and pumpkins, and tobacco, which they likewise cultivate. The Indian corn which we saw was at that time about two feet high, some of it as high as three. The beans were beginning to flower, as also the pumpkins and squashes. They plant their corn in May, and gather it in September.

In addition to cultivation the French assumed that those natives were sedentary because of the existence of a large cabin surrounded by a palisade which the French thought to be a fort.

With the trials of the recent disastrous winter still foremost in their minds, the French judged the Saco region to be ". . . milder and better than . . . where we passed the winter, and at the other places we visited on the coast" on the bases of permanent habitation, agriculture, and "fine trees" of the region. However, they thought that it might be colder than its latitude warranted because ". . . the forests in the interior are very thin. . . ." The party left the Saco area with the thought that the small island at the river's mouth would be a satisfactory site for the post ". . . where one could be in security, " another example of the persistent preference for an insular site in spite of the St. Croix experience.[29]

South of the Saco River the French observed only flatish, sandy coast until the party reached Cape Ann.[30] The French missed the mouths of the Piscataqua and Merrimack rivers. At Cape Ann Champlain recorded his first use of another technique to obtain information from the natives. He drew a map of the cape to which the Indians added the outline of Massachusetts Bay around which they placed six pebbles to indicate the six tribes there and also drew in the Merrimack which the French had missed. Those natives told that they were cultivators. The north shore of Massachusetts Bay was considered pleasant and agreeable, for the French saw many vines and abundant forests as well as much cleared land planted with corn.[31]

During a brief landing the French party encountered another cultural practice of the natives which they had not seen before in

[29] Ibid., Vol. II, p. 67.

[30] Ibid., Vol. II, p. 69. His description of the coast here resembles the Wonderstrands of the Vinland Sagas. See Magnusson, M., and Palsson, H. (trans.), The Vinland Sagas: The Norse Discovery of America (Baltimore: Penguin Books, 1965), p. 94.

[31] Champlain's Voyages, Vol. II, pp. 71-73; Bishop, op. cit., p. 79.

addition to evidence of native commerce. The Indians to that point had used birch bark canoes. At Cape Ann the French found the Indians making and using dugout canoes.[32]

> They are made in the following manner. After cutting down, at a cost of much labor and time, the largest and tallest tree they can find, by means of stone hackets (for they have no others except some few which they received from the savages on the coasts of La Cadie, who obtained them in exchange for furs), they remove the bark, and round off the trees except on one side, where they apply fire gradually along its entire length; and sometimes they put red-hot pebble-stones on top. When the fire is too fierce, they extinguish it with a little water, not entirely, but so that the edge of the boat may not be burnt. It being hollowed out as much as they wish, they scrape it all over with stones, which they use instead of knives. These stones resemble our musket flints.

The Frenchmen tarried off the forested islands of Boston harbor only long enough to verify that they were as the Cape Ann Indians had described and to conclude erroneously that the Charles River was a broad stream which stretched to the lands of the Iroquois. The image of the area being well populated was reenforced by the many canoes of Indians which came out to the French from the islands and mainland. At Brant Point, called Cape St. Louis by de Monts, the French barque ran aground a rock. After it was pulled off and anchored safely, fifteen or sixteen canoes of natives joined them. On the shore were ". . . a great many little houses, scattered over the fields where they plant their corn."[33]

Continuing the journey along the sandy coast of Massachusetts Bay where they saw ". . . great many cabins and gardens . . . ," the French met a small group of Indians who were fishing for cod by means of wooden hooks with spear like bone heads attached by hemp cord. They indicated that the rope was from a wild plant. The French accepted an invitation to visit the river where the natives dwelt, but the boat was unable to enter the small bay at low tide. Champlain went ashore and reported that there was no river, only a small arm of the bay into which an unnavigable brook flowed. The surrounding land was partially cleared. The bay itself was shallow and at places dry during low tide. On one side of its entrance was a low forested point with extensive sand dunes. The French named the bay Port du Cap St. Louis.[34] It is known

---

[32] Champlain's Voyages, Vol. II, pp. 73-74.

[33] Ibid., Vol. II, pp. 75-76.

[34] Ibid., Vol. II, pp. 77-78.

today as Plymouth, the site of the first successful English settlement on the New England coast.

The northern head of Cape Cod was called Cap Blanc because of the whitish appearance given to it by the sand. Behind its treeless sandy shore, dunes, and cliffs were woods ". . . which are very attractive and beautiful. "[35] The French did not land on the Cape until they reached Nauset on the eastern shore. Before arrival there they had their first experience with the dangerous shoal ridden outer waters of the Cape.

Entrance into Nauset was difficult because of the shallow water of low tide. Inside, however, the shore was lined with Indian wigwams and fields. "It would be a very fine place, if the harbor were good." It was named Port du Malebarre and described as "here great quantity of Grapes, . . . a Countrey very full of people." The Nauset wigwams had reed thatch instead of bark or skin cover. Two features of native agriculture previously unseen by the French were observed. The Nauset Indians staggered their planting in order to vary the harvest periods. Uncultivated fields, lying fallow, were burned and then worked with a wooden spade before planting. Attempts to get information about the winter were frustrated by the language barrier. By signs some Indians showed the French that the snow got at least a foot thick; others informed them that it was less and that the harbor never froze. Champlain concluded that the area was mild and did not have a severe winter.[36]

The Indians took a kettle from the French and during the theft killed one Frenchman. De Monts wisely refrained from executing an Indian captive in revenge. But as the first episode of French-native conflicts, it marked the beginning of an image of the southern New England Indians as deceitful, unreliable, and thieving.[37] The second survey ended at Nauset. Fogs, storms, and depleted provisions prompted the return to St. Croix Island. In spite of the favorable descriptions of some places which the French had visited on that traverse, they rejected every site for reasons

---

[35] Ibid., Vol. II, pp. 79-80.

[36] Ibid., Vol. II, pp. 81-83; Levermore, op. cit., Vol. I, p. 267.

[37] Champlain's Voyages, Vol. II, pp. 83-84.

which were not always stated by the chroniclers of the expedition. The purpose of the survey remained undone on their return--". . . to find another place more favorable for our settlement, as we had not been able to do on any of the coasts which we had explored on this voyage."[38]

The third coastal survey, begun on September 5, 1606, was to seek the desired site south of Nauset. But valuable time was wasted by following cautiously the course of the second trip, a route selected over the objections of Champlain who wanted to sail directly to Nauset from the Maine coast. Still the journey had its rewards, for at St. Croix Island the sight of their abandoned crops ". . . gave us great satisfaction to see that the soil there was good and fertile." The revisit to the Isle of Bacchus as its grapes were ripening became authority to claim that they were the equal of French ones and would produce wine.[39]

Gloucester harbor, which had been by-passed earlier, was entered. There the Frenchmen saw additional evidence of Indian agriculture, and a large Indian settlement with nearby meadows ". . . capable of supporting a large number of cattle." The harbor itself appeared big enough to shelter many vessels. Pleasantries of the location, however, were marred by the actions of the natives who appeared somewhat hostile to the strangers.[40] Although the visitors left without an outbreak of hostilities, the unsatisfactory character of the southern New England natives loomed even more negative in the developing French image of the coast.

Climax of the increasingly tense relations with the Indians of southern New England was reached in a battle with a tribe on the southern shore of Cape Cod.[41] After successfully navigating through the Cape's shallow shoal-ridden outer waters, the French party rounded Monomoy Point and landed somewhere on the shores of the Town of Chatham. There the French noted the ". . . considerable quantity of land cleared up, and many little hills, where they cultivated corn and various grains on which they live." To

---

[38]Ibid., Vol. II, p. 90.

[39]Ibid., Vol. II, pp. 109-10; Levermore, op. cit., Vol. I, p. 256.

[40]Champlain's Voyages, Vol. II, pp. 111-14.

previous accounts of Indian agricultural practices was added a
description of winter storage. "All the inhabitants of this place
are very fond of agriculture, and provide themselves with Indian
corn for the winter, which they store in the following manner:
They make trenches in the sand on the slopes of the hills, some
five to six feet deep, more or less. Putting their corn and other
grains into large grass sacks, they throw them into these trenches,
and cover them with sand three or four feet above the surface of
the earth, taking it out as their needs require. In this way, it is
preserved as well as it would be possible to do in our granaries."[42]
In addition to being cultivators, the natives were good fishermen
but poor hunters. Their houses were circular grass or corn
thatched wigwams which were dispersed among their fields. Like
the other Massachusetts tribes whom the French had seen, they
wore skins or leaves rather than furs.[43] In general Champlain
thought the area ". . . would be an excellent place to erect buildings and lay the foundations of a state, if the harbor were somewhat deeper and the entrance safer."[44]

After a stay of eight or nine days during which the natives
seemed friendly, the French observed the natives on the move into
the woods. A small band of the French who refused to obey the
captain's orders to retire on board the ship were attacked by the
Indians. The French returning from the ship finally drove off the
attackers, but there were casualties on both sides. The French
then sailed westward along the low sandy south coast of the Cape
possibly as far as Buzzards Bay where contrary winds forced them
to return to the site of the battle. It marked the southern and
westernmost limit of French survey of the New England coast.[45]

The French returned to their base camp at Port Royal via the
shorter direct route across the Gulf of Maine to the islands between

---

[41] See Levermore, op. cit., Vol. I, pp. 267-74, for Lescarbot's version of the fight.

[42] Champlain's Voyages, Vol. II, p. 121.   [43] Ibid., Vol. II, pp. 123-24.

[44] Ibid., Vol. II, p. 126.

[45] Bishop, op. cit., pp. 99-100; Champlain's Voyages, Vol. II, pp. 126-30; Levermore, op. cit., Vol. I, p. 275.

the mouths of the Kennebec and the Penobscot.[46] With that retreat
French effort to find a satisfactory location for a fur station on
the New England coast ended. The de Monts group withdrew eventually from Nova Scotia as well as New England.[47] Shortly there-
after Champlain undertook the settlement of Quebec and established
the beginnings of French activities there as they would function
until expelled by the Treaty of Paris 1763. Although each of the
surveys sponsored by de Monts was a failure in that no fur station
site was considered satisfactory, the experience gained by Champlain during those surveys was utilized to positive value in the
development of Quebec.[48]

After the efforts of de Monts collapsed the French made no
attempt to reestablish a major focus of fur trading on the New
England coast. The persistence and tenacity which they later displayed in Quebec were not applied to New England because of the
negative image which developed from the de Monts experience, in
spite of the many favorable characteristics which were encountered
during the surveys. The loss of the monopoly by de Monts might
be partial explanation for an interruption of French activities, but
it is not sufficient to account for total abandonment.[49] Other sponsors could have filled the void; instead the French chose to focus
their efforts elsewhere in an area more satisfactory for their
purpose.

De Monts hoped to develop a systematic fur trade. He was
not interested in duplicating the contemporary practice and organization of occasional ships sailing to a coast and trading wherever
and whenever the natives were willing. He planned commerce on a
sustained basis which required a well placed permanent post in a
region where furs could be collected and shipped over a long period
of time. It was against that conception of the fur trade that the
characteristics of early seventeenth century New England must be
judged in order to understand its rejection and the French preference for the St. Lawrence Valley.

---

[46] Champlain's Voyages, Vol. II, pp. 136-37; Levermore, op. cit., Vol. I, p. 276.

[47] Clark, A. H., Acadia: The Geography of Early Nova Scotia to 1760 (Madison:
(University of Wisconsin Press, 1968), pp. 78-79.

[48] Levermore, op. cit., Vol. I, p. 219.   [49] Ibid., Vol. I, pp. 287-88.

The choice of a location where the functions of a continuing fur station could be performed was dependent on local and regional characteristics. The principal necessities of the post's site were a commodious harbor, deep enough to accommodate ocean ships, with a non-hazardous entrance defensible from land and sea attacks, and with access to fur producing areas. Immediate requirements of the site included timber for fuel and construction, potable water, and adequate space for buildings and post activities. The criterion of defense had to be adjusted to the accessibility demand, for the post would not function as intended if it was isolated from distant or nearby fur collecting areas. Access to as large a collection area as possible imposed a location on or near a stream with a sizable drainage basin, "for the roads in that country are the rivers and the sea."[50]

An obvious regional criterion was the abundant presence of fur bearing animals of species whose pelts were marketable in France. The number of such animals in any area would be governed by ecological conditions in which a large agricultural population using fire to clear land would be a detrimental factor. The modern researcher is grateful to Champlain for his descriptions of Indian agriculture, but it is questionable that men seeking areas with numerous fur animals would interpret those characteristics positively because of the implied reduction of available pelts. It is thus significant that in his descriptions of the region south of the Saco River fur bearing animals were not mentioned, probably because they were not seen. Their scarcity was further suggested by their absence from native dress.[51]

Although too sizable a native population of agricultural habits was detrimental to the fur trade, some natives were necessary to the system as de Monts envisioned it, for they were intended to be the principal hunters and collectors of the furs. South of the Saco River the natives appeared to have little interest in hunting and to be poor practitioners of it. The proposed system based as it was on native hunting depended also on their cooperation and willingness

---

[50]Innes, op. cit., pp. 5-6; Thwaites, R. G. (ed.), The Jesuit Relations and Allied Documents (New York: Pageant Book Company, 1959), Vol. III, p. 257.

[51]Bishop, op. cit., p. 81.

to comply with French demands. The three hostile occurrences
with different indigenous groups were convincing evidence that they
were not docile and would attempt to overwhelm strangers. Under
such conditions the danger to a small French outpost increased as
the size of the Indian population increased. An area with a large
agricultural population was not only potentially more dangerous but
also less apt to be worth the risks because of limited productivity
of furs.

The severe winters, one of which was so critical in the abandonment of the only post which de Monts' group established in New
England, seemed not to be an important long range consideration.
Winter conditions in the Quebec region which the French ultimately
selected were at best equal to northern Maine, if not worse. Perhaps the reduced incidence of illness the second winter at Port
Royal had convinced the French that the occurrence of scurvy was
less intense at slightly higher latitudes.

In 1613 the French attempted to reverse their previous total
rejection of the coast and had assessed the northern part of Maine
satisfactory for another purpose--a Jesuit mission. Renewed
French consideration of the New England coast was associated with
their return to Acadia with Port Royal again as the center; the New
England coast was only peripherally involved. Visits were made
sporadically to the coast by fur traders and to obtain corn. Dis-
concerted by tales of the English there, the French viewed the
region as a buffer zone where it was to their interests in Acadia to
exclude or control anything the English might attempt.

The important new element in the second phase of French
activity on the New England coast was the presence of Catholic mis-
sionaries who were to convert the natives to Christianity and to
establish missions around which the natives could be gathered. A
Jesuit mission was planned and sponsored by the Marquise de
Guercheville who obtained a patent from the king and the cession
of all claims from de Monts. The Jesuits sent by her arrived at
Port Royal on January 23, 1612.[52] However, when Port Royal was
found to be unsatisfactory, the French sponsors sent another ship
from France to remove the Jesuits to a suitable mission site. The

---

[52]Thwaites, op. cit., Vol. II, pp. 231-37.

new location was to have been at the confluence of the Penobscot
and the Kenduskeag rivers near present-day Bangor.[53] After leaving Port Royal with the settlement party, the ship became lost in
fog for two days. When the fogs lifted, the ship was off Mount
Desert Island. "The pilot turned to the Eastern shore of the Island
and there located us in a large and beautiful port . . . we called
this place and port Saint Sauveur."[54]

Natives visited the ship and asked for Father Biard whom they
had met on his trip to the Penobscot two years earlier. Learning
of the French intent to settle on the Penobscot, the natives attempted to convince them that Saint Sauveur was better, more
beautiful, and more healthy than the proposed site. When those
arguments failed to dissuade the French, Father Biard was request-
ed to go to their village and baptize the ill and dying chief. He
was not dying, but the view of the area during the journey to the
village was sufficiently impressive that the French, changing their
minds, decided to establish their settlement nearby. Biard's
description of the site which he selected follows:[55]

This place is a beautiful hill, rising gently from the sea, its sides bathed by two
springs; the land is cleared for twenty or twenty-five acres, and in some places is
covered with grass almost as high as a man. It faces the South and East, and is near
the mouth of the Pentegoet, where several broad and pleasant rivers, which abound in
fish, discharge their waters; its soil is dark, rich and fertile; the Port and Harbor
are as fine as can be seen, and are in a position favorable to command the entire
coast; the Harbor especially is as safe as a pond. For, besides being strengthened by
the great island of Mount desert, it is still more protected by certain small Islands
which break the currents and the winds, and fortify the entrance. There is not a fleet
which it is not capable of sheltering, nor a ship so deep that could not approach within
a cable's length of the shore to unload.

The French disputed among themselves whether first to begin
cultivation of crops as the ship's captain desired or to build houses
and fortifications as the Jesuit fathers wanted. The latter won the
argument; although quarrels continued, the buildings were started.
The quarrels and construction stopped abruptly when ". . . the
English brought us all to an understanding with each other. . . ."[56]

---

[53]Ibid., Vol. II, p. 249, Vol. III, pp. 261-63; Levermore, op. cit., Vol. II, p. 551.

[54]Thwaites, op. cit., Vol. III, p. 265. The harbor is now known as Frenchman's Bay.

[55]Ibid., Vol. III, pp. 269-71. Many of these characteristics were also criteria for a
fur trading post.

[56]Ibid., Vol. III, p. 273, Vol. IV, p. 9.

It has been noted at the beginning of this chapter that French and English interests in the New England coast revived simultaneously at the start of the seventeenth century. Initially English presence was marked solely by expeditions sent directly from England. Although there was yet no martial confrontation between these competitors on the coast, each was aware in some fashion of the other's activities. For example, de Monts learned of Waymouth's visit shortly after the English ship departed. The French had a distorted version of the Popham colony and had visited its abandoned fort on an expedition sent from Port Royal to get corn from the Massachusetts Indians and to investigate the rumors and reports of the English activities.[57] As parties of each country came more frequently to the coast, engagement between them was inevitable.

When the salvo of imperial conflict sounded on the coast, it involved colonials rather than direct agents of the mother countries. On the English side were Virginians who had begun to fish in New England waters to supplement their colony's precarious food supplies. While Biard and the French argued how to initiate the Mount Desert mission, a Virginian vessel commanded by Captain Samuel Argall unaware both of and to the French anchored nearby. Informed of the French construction by natives who thought that the English were French, Argall attacked and captured the entire French party, its ships, and equipment. The Virginians burned the French camp, released some of the prisoners, but carried others including the Jesuits captive to Virginia from whence they were transported to England.[58]

---

[57] Brown, Alexander, The Genesis of the United States (New York: Russell & Russell, 1964), Vol. II, pp. 533-36.

[58] Thwaites, op. cit., Vol. III, pp. 7-9, 275-83, Vol. IV, pp. 9-37; Levermore, op. cit., Vol. II, pp. 551-52; Arber, E. (ed.), Travels and Works of Captain John Smith (Edinburgh: John Grant, 1910), Vol. II, p. 517; Parkman, Francis, Pioneers of France in the New World (Boston: Little, Brown, 1931), pp. 312-13. Authorities differ on their interpretations of Argall's mission. Some claim that he was fishing, a purpose which leaves unanswered why his ship was so well armed; others stated that he was sent to remove any and all poachers whom he found within the limits of English title, a motive which presumes that the governor of Virginia might have exceeded his authority. Another interpretation is that he was both fishing and protecting English interests. His later burning of Port Royal was under the commission of the governor of Virginia. See Baxter, J. P. (ed), Sir Ferdinando Gorges and His Province of Maine (Boston: Prince Society, 1890),

The authority for Argall's attack on the French was that they were within the area assigned to the second (Plymouth) company by James I.[59] It was left to the English government to resolve the diplomatic tempest caused by Argall's bold enforcement of England's territorial claims and to placate the French. For the while the Virginians were left in possession of an area which they had no title to, did not occupy, and little frequented.

After the incipient Jesuit mission in Maine and Acadia was dissolved, Father Biard interpreted the events which caused its destruction and his capture. ". . . It must be understood that the English do not dispute with us all of new France. For they dare not refuse what everybody grants us, but they only contest some of the boundaries. They grant us then a new France, but bound it by the shores of the Gulf and great river Saint Lawrence, and restrict us within the 47th, 48th and 49th degrees of north latitude. At least they do not allow us to go farther south than the forty-sixth degree. . . ."[60] He exhorted his countrymen to challenge the English and press their claims to the 39th parallel. He offered de jure arguments in the face of English de facto success. Among the ten points on which he based his case for French sovereignty was, "Everyone knows this through the voyages of Champlain, for he relates in these that, in the year 1607, sieur de Monts was at Port Royal, and, through his people and authority, ruled all the country to the 39th degree as Lieutenant of his most Christian Majesty."[61] His rhetoric was for lawyers, not the men of action who struggled in the New World. For history the French failure to establish a foothold in New England was as prophetic of their ulti-

---

Vol. I, pp. 207-8; Brown, op. cit., Vol. II, p. 662; Calendar of State Papers, op. cit., Vol. I, p. 15; Deane, Charles, "Documents Relating to the Expeditions of Captain Samuel Argall," Proceedings of the Massachusetts Historical Society, 2nd Series, I (1884-85), 187-92; Hamor, Ralph, A True Discourse of the Present State of Virginia (London: John Beals, 1615), pp. 36-37; Howe, Henry F., Prologue to New England (New York: Farrar and Rinehart, 1943), pp. 205-18; O'Callaghan, E. B. (ed.), Documents Relative to the Colonial History of the State of New York (Albany: Weed, Parsons and Company, 1853), Vol. III, pp. 1-2; Sir William Alexander and American Colonization (Boston: Prince Society, 1873), pp. 181-84; Thwaites, op. cit., Vol. IV, pp. 39-49.

[59] Calendar of State Papers, op. cit., Vol. I, p. 6.

[60] Thwaites, op. cit., Vol. IV, pp. 99-101.

[61] Ibid., Vol. IV, p. 103.

mate exclusion from the continent as was the English victory in that first conflict prophetic of the final English supremacy. What had been rejected for the fur trade the French would not reclaim from the English for empire or Catholicism.

CHAPTER IV

NORTH VIRGINIA:

FISH, FURS, AND COLONIAL FAILURE

The cod which became the symbol of colonial Massachusetts because of the wealth and well being which its sale brought to the colony could partially symbolize the riches which the English hoped to get from the New England coast when they returned to it at the beginning of the seventeenth century. It has been noted that French and English interest in the coast revived simultaneously at that time. Each was motivated for the most part by hopes of mercantile gains, but each differed in the choice of commodity which was the focus of the hoped-for exploitation. The French stressed furs, while the English put greater emphasis on the sea than on products of the land. Other motives such as the search for the Northwest Passage, precious metals, and the spread of Christianity were recurring but minor factors.

New World fisheries of the North Atlantic had been used as a general argument to promote English activities in overseas adventures for over a century before it was crystalized as the most promotable item of the New England region. A variety of factors encouraged the focus of some Englishmen in the New England fisheries. The market for a cheap and volume marketable fish, not only in England but also on the continent, created demand for which the English were only one supplier. Problems of access for English fishermen to the Icelandic fishing grounds were old by the time of Columbus' discovery. Portuguese, Basque, Breton, and Spanish fishermen who used the Newfoundland fishery were not much impressed by Gilbert's claim of the area for England. One solution to these difficulties in line with the thinking of the times was to find a satisfactory fishing area which would be exclusively English. The search for such an area led some English promoters, particularly ones trying to compete with the traditional fish merchants, to investigate the credentials of New England.

English efforts to remove the New England coast from the veil of myth and ignorance in which it lingered after Gilbert's rash failure began as the reign of Elizabeth I was nearing its close. The Earl of Southampton, a prisoner for his role in the Essex conspiracy, commissioned Bartholomew Gosnold and Bartholomew Gilbert to explore the coast and establish a small colony. On March 26, 1602, Gosnold's ship sailed from Falmouth, a symbolic association with earlier ventures, for it was the harbor into which the remains of Gilbert's fleet had limped.[1]

The location of Gosnold's landfall on the New England coast is disputed with agreement only that it was north of Cape Cod. His most comprehensive biographer argued that it was Cape Neddick on the southern Maine coast.[2] Other selections are somewhere in Maine between Portland and Kittery, Cape Ann, Salem harbor, or Cape Cod. The succinct description of the rocky headland at 43°N seems more appropriate for the Maine coast than a more southern choice.[3] The expedition immediately encountered evidence that other Europeans had preceded them to this coast. A Basque fishing vessel came out from the shore, but it was manned by Indians who wore various pieces of European clothing, spoke a few European words, drew a chalk map of the coast, knew of Placentia Bay in Newfoundland, and seemed to understand much of what the English said to them.[4] For reasons not made clear in the narratives

---

[1]Burrage, Henry S., The Beginnings of Colonial Maine 1602-1658 (Augusta: for the State of Maine, 1914), p. 19; Gookin, W. F., Bartholomew Gosnold (Hamden, Conn.: Archon Books, 1963), p. 83; Howe, Henry F., Prologue to New England (New York: Farrar & Rinehart, 1943), p. 55; and Preston, R. A., Gorges of Plymouth Fort (Toronto: University of Toronto Press, 1953), p. 138.

[2]Gookin, op. cit., p. 87.

[3]Palfrey, J. G., History of New England (Boston: Little, Brown, 1858), Vol. I, p. 71; Stith, William, The History of the First Discovery and Settlement of Virginia (Williamsburg: William Parks, 1747), p. 31; and Weeden, W. B., Economic and Social History of New England 1620-1789 (Boston: Houghton, Mifflin, 1890), Vol. I, p. 9. See Burrage, op. cit., p. 20, for analysis of the limited evidence favoring a Maine landfall.

[4]The two sources of the Gosnold voyage are Archer, Gabriel, "The Relation of Captaine Gosnols Voyage to the North Part of Virginia," in Purchas, S., Hakluytus Posthumus or Purchas His Pilgrimes (New York: AMS Press, 1965), Vol. XVIII, pp. 302-13, and

Gosnold left the coast immediately. Perhaps the European para-
phernalia worn by the natives suggested hostile treatment of previous European visitors or the presence of European competitors
for native trade, either circumstance not propitious for the small
colony which was to be established. Archer implied that the ship
had been ordered to a specific site or to one with characteristics
not found at the landfall.[5] Brereton's explanation that there were
no satisfactory harbors was out of character with the usual statements of the abundance of good harbors to be used on the Maine
coast.[6]

Cape Cod was sighted during the day after departure from the
Maine coast, and the ship anchored somewhere along its north and
west coast.[7] Gosnold and a small party went ashore--the landing
site is unknown, the first indisputable instance of the Cape's exploration by Europeans. Brereton, who was one of the shore party,
told little of what was seen except that the vista from a hill proved
". . . this headland to be a parcell of the maine. . . ."[8] Archer
related a few more details. "The Captaine went here ashoare and
found the ground to be full of Pease, Strawberies, Hurtberies, &,
as then unripe; the sand also by the shoare somewhat deepe, the
firewood there by us taken in was of Cypresse, Birch, Wich-Hazell
and Beech. A young Indian came here to the captaine armed with
his Bow and Arrowes, and had certaine plates of Copper hanging at
his Eares; hee shewed a willingnesse to help us in our occasions."[9]

While the party had been exploring ashore, the men on the
ship fished. Of the sight of the deck covered with fish Brereton
with a true promoter's instinct linked the destiny of the coast to

---

Brereton, John, A Briefe and True Relation of Discouerie of the North Part of Virginia
(London: Geor. Bishop, 1602). Both of these have been reprinted several times. The
citations here are to the annotated versions which appear in Levermore, C. H. (ed.),
Forerunners and Competitors of the Pilgrims and Puritans (Brooklyn: New England Society
of Brooklyn, 1912), Vol. I, pp. 31-42 (Brereton) and pp. 43-54 (Archer). See Levermore,
op. cit., Vol. I, pp. 32, 44-45.

[5]Levermore, op. cit., Vol. I, p. 45.

[6]Ibid., Vol. I, p. 32; Strachey, William, The Historie of Travell into Virginia
Britania (London: Hakluyt Society, 1952), p. 152.

[7]Levermore, op. cit., Vol. I, pp. 32, 45.

[8]Ibid., Vol. I, p. 32.   [9]Ibid., Vol. I, pp. 45-46.

the cod fishery and presented the often repeated claim that it was
better than Newfoundland. ". . . In five or six hours absence, we
had pestered our ship so with Cod fish, that we threw them over-
boord againe; and surely, I am persuaded that in the moneths of
March, April, and May, there is upon this coast better fishing,
and in as great plentie, as in Newfound-land: for the sculles of
Mackerell, Herrings, Cod and other fish, that we dayly saw as we
went and came from the shore were woonderfull; and besides, the
places where we tooke these Cods (and might in a few daies have
laden our ship) were but in seven fadome water, and within lesse
than a league of the shore; where, in Newfound-land they fish in
fortie or fiftie fadome water, and farre off."[10] The headland
where that bounty of the sea was caught was appropriately named
Cape Cod.[11] The ship then sailed around the cape which was
described as a low, wooded land.[12]

Although the remainder of the voyage was outside the limits
defined for this study, it introduced themes which were important
to the study area and hence is considered here. The course of the
ship after rounding the southern end of Cape Cod can not be identified with certitude because both Archer and Brereton were extremely vague at that point in their narratives.[13] The expedition was to
plant a colony somewhere along the coast and part of the crew left
to staff it.

Gosnold named the island which he selected for the colony
Elizabeth's Isle, which is usually assumed to be Cuttyhunk, although
the present-day landscape has little resemblance to the descriptions of Archer and Brereton.[14] To them the island was well-
wooded with various species including sassafras, had plenty of

[10] Ibid., Vol. I, pp. 32-33; Strachey, op. cit., pp. 152-53. See "Tracts Appended to Brereton," Collections of Massachusetts Historical Society, 3rd Series, Vol. VIII, pp. 93-100, for Brereton's promotional use of the New England fisheries. His promotional activity is discussed in Taylor, E. G. R., Late Tudor and Early Stuart Geography 1583-1650 (New York: Octagon Books, 1968), p. 158.

[11] Levermore, op. cit., Vol. I, p. 45.   [12] Ibid., Vol. I, p. 33.

[13] See frontispiece map in Gookin, op. cit., for his conjectural route of the voyage after departure from the Maine coast.

[14] Burrage, op. cit., p. 21; Gookin, op. cit., p. 142.

fresh water, abounded with game and fowl, and possessed soil
". . . in comparison whereof, the most fertil part of al England is
. . . but barren. . . ."[15] On Elizabeth's Isle Gosnold chose a
situation for his fort with characteristics which would not be immediately duplicated. He built the post on a small islet in an inland
pond away from the ocean.[16] Brereton's assertion that the crew's
reaction to the island was like men beholding a paradise was inconsistent with their refusal to stay at the fort as planned. With their
refusal the first English colonial expedition to reach successfully
the New England coast failed in its purpose.[17]

As the expedition passed along the southern coast of the Cape
evidence of a large Indian population was observed. Unlike Champlain a few years later, Archer considered them to be timorous,
but they both eventually agreed that the natives were "very theev-
ish."[18] In spite of the stress on cod as the profitable commodity
to be obtained from the New England coast, other items filled the
hold of Gosnold's ship when it returned. Furs and skins had been
bartered from the natives at the Elizabeth's Isle Fort. Sassafras,
however, proved to be the most profitable item in an England which
believed it to have miraculous curative powers.[19]

Although the colonial portion of Gosnold's journey was a failure, its commercial aspects were successful enough to be the
impetus for another group of sponsors to dispatch a vessel to the
New England coast. The evidence of Gosnold's marketable cargo,
the reports of teeming schools of fish related by Robert Salterne,

---

[15] Levermore, op. cit., Vol. I, p. 36.

[16] Ibid., Vol. I, pp. 37, 49; Strachey, op. cit., p. 154.

[17] Levermore, op. cit., Vol. I, pp. 41, 54; Strachey, op. cit., pp. 154-55. Greed
of the men who wanted their shares of the cargo was the motive for the refusal to stay in
these chronicles. Brereton by ascribing the action to the crew's cupidity also enhanced
the value of the cargo in the eyes of his contemporaries. He was astute to use the expedition's failure to promotional advantage.

[18] Levermore, op. cit., Vol. I, pp. 46-47.

[19] Ibid., Vol. I, pp. 41, 54; Gookin, op. cit., pp. 158-59. See Monardes, Nicholas,
and Frampton, John, Joyfull Newes out of the Newe Founde Worlde (New York: Alfred A.
Knopf, 1925 [reprint of 1577 London edition]), Vol. I, pp. 99ff., for the esteem in which
sassafras was held as a medicinal drug.

and the influence of Richard Hakluyt persuaded a group of leading
Bristol merchants to sponsor ". . . a Voyage for the farther Discoverie of the North part of Virginia."[20] The ship left Bristol on
March 20, 1603, under the command of Martin Pring who was the
last Elizabethan adventurer on the coast and the first Jacobean one,
for the great Queen died while the ship was becalmed in Milford
Haven.[21]

Pring's ship reached the New England coast somewhere among
the islands east of Penobscot Bay. These he assessed as a future
site of fishing operations. "Heere wee found in excellent fishing
for Cods, which are better then those of New-found-land, and withall we saw good and Rockie ground fit to drie them upon: also we
see no reason to the contrary, but that Salt may bee made in these
parts, a matter of no small importance."[22] He moved southward
and entered four inlets where he encountered two principal objections: shallow bars and streams which did not seem to go far into
the interior.[23] To that point in his journey Pring had seen no
natives, only evidence of their existence. He recorded the various
species of trees and animals which he recognized but left the area
after a brief non-communicative meeting with some Indians because
". . . we could find no Sassafras."[24] Thus, the purpose of his
mission was certain.

From Savage Rock, perhaps Cape Neddick, the ship sailed
into Massachusetts Bay, ". . . that great Gulfe which Captaine

---

[20]The narrative of Pring's voyage is found in Purchas, op. cit., Vol. XVIII, pp.
322-29. Salterne had been on Gosnold's expedition and may have been an agent for the
Bristol group which sponsored Pring with whom he returned to New England. See MacInnes,
C. M., A Gateway of Empire (Bristol: J. W. Arrowsmith, 1939), p. 69.

[21]Purchas, op. cit., Vol. XVIII, p. 323. For data on Pring consult Pring, James H.,
Captain Martin Pringe: The Last of the Elizabethan Seamen (Plymouth, U.K.: W. H. Luke,
1888), and Tercentenary of Martin Pring's First Voyage to the Coast of Maine 1603-1903
(Portland: Maine Historical Society, 1905).

[22]Purchas, op. cit., Vol. XVIII, p. 323.

[23]Ibid., Vol. XVIII, pp. 323-24. One editor thought these four inlets to be the mouths
of the Saco, Kennebunk, York, and Piscataqua rivers. Although Pring himself was silent
on the matter, the concern about openings into the interior suggests that he was looking for
evidence of a northwest passage. See Levermore, op. cit., Vol. I, p. 62.

[24]Purchas, op. cit., Vol. XVIII, p. 324.

Gosnold overshot the yeere before. . . ." There Pring saw on the north shore natives but no sassafras. So he moved to the south shore of the bay where he entered an inlet which ". . . had sufficient quantitie of Sassafras." The small bay was named Whitson Bay for the mayor of Bristol and a small hill near the shore Mount Aldworth for a principal sponsor.[25] A camp was established, and the crew set to collecting sassafras. The area was well populated with natives who visited the camp in large numbers. The Indians enjoyed the guitar playing and singing of a crew lad but were frightened by the dogs. Fish seemed the mainstay of the local diet, although patches of maize, tobacco, and other plants and their use of skins for clothing indicated that they were agriculturists and hunters as well as fishermen. They made birch-bark canoes. They were both taller and larger bodied than the English. But despite their physical attractiveness and naive delight with European music, Pring considered them treacherous.[26]

To test the area's suitability for English crops Pring's group prepared small plots of ground by shovelling and planted wheat, barley, oats, peas, and other unidentified seeds which ". . . came up well, giving certaine testimonie of the goodnesse of the climate and of the Soyle." On the basis of that experiment and of the presence of wild grasses Pring concluded that ". . . Hempe, Flaxe, Rape-seed, and such like which require a rich and fat ground, would prosper excellently in these parts."

The abundance of sassafras had determined the place where Pring's party would sojourn for seven weeks to collect a cargo. But he also recorded the presence of other familiar species such as oak, beech, and birch and some unknown to him. Among the fruit and nut bearing species he noted hazel, cherry, walnut, plum, and maple trees. The witch-hazel was called ". . . the best wood of all other to make Sope-ashes. . . ." He repeated the pattern of

---

[25] Ibid., Vol. XVIII, p. 324. Pring's description of the site and its location suggest that it is the Plymouth of Pilgrim fame. However, on the Velasco map the name Whitsons Bay was given to all of Massachusetts Bay, not restricted to a small inlet. The northern end of Cape Cod was called Whitsons Head, and the Cape's southern point alone was labeled Cape Cod.

[26] Ibid., Vol. XVIII, pp. 324-26. Note that Champlain did not encounter the use of birch-bark canoes this far south. The bay area was perhaps at that time a transitional

emphasis on the familiar and usable in his description of fauna and stressed the animals ". . . whose Cases and Furres being hereafter purchased by exchange may yeeld no smal gaine to us. " The land around his Whitson Bay was ". . . full of Gods good blessings. . . ."

However impressed Pring was with the potential bounty of the land he ended his catalog of the country's economic virtues with the produce of the sea. ". . . So is the sea replenished with great abundance of excellent fish, as Cods sufficient to lade many ships, which we found upon the Coast in the moneth of June, Seales to make Oile withall, Mullets, Turbuts, Mackerels, Herrings, Crabs, Lobsters, Crevises, and Muscles with ragged Pearles in them. "[27] The absence of interest in colonization or assessment of the coast as the seat of an English colony from Pring's voyage narrative illustrates the narrow image of the New England coast held in the Bristol commercial group during that period. The focus was on the immediately exploitable, not the long term benefits of colonies. Although Hakluyt, honored as the father of English colonization, was instrumental in initiating Pring's voyage, he was unable to move the Bristol supporters beyond commercial involvement in North America.

Captain George Waymouth was sent to search for a northwest passage but instead explored part of the New England coast. The sponsors of the expedition were the Earl of Southampton, recently released from the Tower by Elizabeth I's successor, James I, and his Catholic brother-in-law, Baron Arundell of Wardour. Part of the original purpose of the voyage may have been to explore south of the area surveyed in 1602 by Gosnold, also sponsored by Southampton, but Gorges claimed that Waymouth was sent on a search for the passage but explored the New England coast when it was apparent that the original mission could not be accomplished.[28] On

---

[27] Ibid., Vol. XVIII, pp. 327-28.

[28] Gorges, Ferdinando, A Briefe Narration of the Originall Undertakings of the Advancement of Plantations into the Parts of America in Baxter, J. P. (ed.), Sir Ferdinando Gorges and His Province of Maine (Boston: Prince Society, 1890), Vol. II, pp. 7-8; Preston, op. cit., p. 138. Gorges was not a sponsor of this voyage as some have claimed, although its results were critical to his later efforts. Arundell lost interest in the affair before the ship returned and entered Spanish service in the Netherlands. Southampton was to play a prominent role in the Virginia Company.

May 15, 1605, Waymouth's ship sighted Sankaty Head on Nantucket.
Unable to land because of shoals and unable to proceed south or
west because of contrary winds, the ship was driven northward
until on May 17 land was resighted. [29]

The ship had reached Monhegan Island, Maine. After the
storm tossed voyage it appeared a pleasant haven. "This Iland is
woody, grouen with Firre, Birch, Oke and Beech, as farre as we
saw along the shore; and so likely to be within. On the verge grow
Gooseberries, Strawberries, Wild pease and Wild rose bushes. The
water issued foorth downe the Rocky cliffes in many places: and
much fowle of divers kinds breed upon the shore and rocks." The
crew duplicated Gosnold's achievement in catching fish. "While we
were at shore, our men aboord with a few hooks got above thirty
great Cods and Hadocks, which gave us a taste of the great plenty
of fish which we found afterward wheresoever we went upon the
coast." Although "very high mountaines" were seen on the mainland, its generally low profile was considered an omen for the discovery of good land there. [30]

Waymouth chose not to linger at Monhegan and searched among
the St. George's Islands for a satisfactory anchorage. St. George's
harbor was selected and named Pentecost Harbor. [31] At the camp
site garden seeds, peas, and barley were planted and grew well,
". . . although this was but the crust of the ground, and much
inferior to the mould we after found in the maine." The trees of
the islands, "some very great, and all tall," were birch, beech,
ash, maple, spruce, cherry, yew, oak, and "Firre-tree, out of
which issueth Turpentine in so marvellous plenty . . . this would

---

[29] Burrage, op. cit., pp. 40-41. The principal primary source for the Waymouth
voyage is James Rosier, A True Relation of a Most Prosperous Voyage Made This Present
Yeere 1605 by Captaine George Waymouth . . . (London: George Bishop, 1605). It was
included in Purchas, op. cit., Vol. XVIII, pp. 335-60; Levermore, op. cit., Vol. I, pp.
308-51; and Burrage, H. S. (ed.), Gorges and the Grant of the Province of Maine 1622
(Augusta: for the State of Maine, 1923). Page citations here refer to the Burrage edition.
See Burrage, Gorges and the Grant, pp. 42-44.

[30] Burrage, Gorges and the Grant, pp. 44-45. These mountains probably are the
Union and Camden Hills, although some interpreters think them to be the White Mountains.
See Burrage, The Beginnings, p. 42.

[31] Burrage, Gorges and the Grant, p. 45. Boothbay Harbor has been suggested as the
location, but Rosier's description fits St. George's Harbor better. See Burrage, The
Beginnings, p. 43.

be a great benefit for making Tarre and Pitch." Rosier thus pre-
dicted the future of Maine forests as producers of naval stores.
Where the trees were not thick, various berries and vines grew.
Attention was given to the fishing. ". . . All the fish, of what
kinde soever we took, were well fed, fat, and sweete in taste."
They repeated Pring's finding of small pearls in mussels. Those
sights so pleased some of the crew that ". . . many of our Com-
panie wished themselves settled heere, not expecting any further
hopes, or better discovery to be made."[32] From it, however,
Waymouth and a small party set out to investigate the mainland.

The characteristics of the natives whom they encountered differed only in small measure from the descriptions of earlier and
later narratives. Instead of being larger than the English as
Pring depicted them, they were ". . . very proportionable . . .
not very tal nor big, but in stature like us." Their clothing, limited as it was, was made of beaver and deer skins. They were
quick, intelligent, and ". . . seemed all very civill and merrie:
shewing tokens of much thankefulnesse, for those things we gave
them." Their canoes were built with "excellent ingenious art."[33]
They were intrigued with European trinkets and small metal items
which Waymouth exchanged for furs. In spite of the generous and
apparently amicable relations between the two groups, the Indians
used a proposed trading rendezvous to prepare an ambush for the
English. But the hidden armed warriors were noticed, and the
usual epithet of treachery was applied to the Indians.[34]

During the explorations of the mainland Waymouth ". . . discovered up a great river, trending alongst into the maine about
forty miles."[35] This stream has been variously identified as the
Penobscot, the Kennebec, or St. George's river. Rosier's descrip-

---

[32] Burrage, Gorges and the Grant, pp. 47-48.

[33] Burrage, Gorges and the Grant, pp. 49-50, 52-55.

[34] Burrage, Gorges and the Grant, pp. 57-59. Rosier informed us that the English
acted well towards the natives only when further contacts were desired. Waymouth kidnapped five Indians before he left. But that odious action did not receive the moral con-
demnation heaped on the Indians for defense of their land and persons.

[35] Burrage, Gorges and the Grant, p. 51; Strachey, op. cit., p. 156.

tion seems best fitted to the last, but the evidence is inconclusive.[36]
Because Rosier considered a long navigable river to be the ". . .
richest treasury to any land," Waymouth's great river evoked com-
parisons with the famed rivers of France and the fabled ones of
South America, all of which were its inferiors. However, it did
not get precedence to England's Thames. "I will not prefer it
before our river of Thames, because it is England's richest treasure; but we all did wish those excellent Harbours, good deeps in a
continuall convenient breadth and small tide-gates, to be as well
therein for our countries good, as we found them here (beyond our
hopes) in certaine, for these to whom it shall please God to grant
this land for habitation; which if it had, with the other inseparable
adherent commodities here to be found; then I would boldly affirme
it to be the most rich, beautifull, large and secure harbouring
river that the world affoordeth."[37]

The land on each side of the stream was equally attractive.
The terrain was level and not rocky. The upland was covered with
a forest of various species which in turn was bordered by grasses.
The trees were tall and usable species which indicated to the be-
holder that the soils were very fertile. Only clearing of the forest was needed to convert the region into productive meadows. And
in some places the forest was thin enough that little labor would be
required for the clearing. Fresh water was abundant throughout
the area.[38]

A journey into the interior provided the basis for a more
specific evaluation of the lands away from the river.

In this march we passed over very good ground, pleasant and fertile, fit for pasture,
for the space of some three miles, having but little wood, and that Oke like stands left

---

[36] Burrage, The Beginnings, p. 46; Coleman, R. V., The First Frontier (New York:
Charles Scribner's Sons, 1948), p. 72; Gilman, Stanwood, and Gilman, Margaret, Land of
the Kennebec (Boston: Branden Press, 1966), p. 23; Howe, op. cit., p. 90; Levermore,
op. cit., Vol. I, p. 326; Palfrey, op. cit., Vol. I, p. 76; Pinkerton, John, A General Col-
lection of the Best and Most Interesting Voyages and Travels in All Parts of the World
(London: Longman, Hurst, Rees, Orme, and Brown, 1812), Vol. XII, pp. 228-29; Sir
William Alexander and American Colonization (Boston: Prince Society, 1873), p. 30;
Stith, op. cit., p. 33.

[37] Burrage, Gorges and the Grant, pp. 62-64. Rosier was too optimistic about the
general sailing conditions on the coast, for he wrote that it was devoid of dangerous rocks.

[38] Ibid., p. 63.

in our pastures in England, good and great, fit timber for any use. Some small Birch, Hazle and Brake, which might in small time with few men by cleansed and made good arable land: but as it now is will feed cattell of all kindes with fodder enough for Summer and Winter. The soile is blacke, bearing sundry hearbs, grasse, and strawberries bigger than ours in England. In many places are lowe Thicks like our Copisses of small yoong wood. And surely it did all resemble a stately Parke, wherein appeare some old trees with high withered tops, and other flourishing with living greene boughs. Upon the hilles grow notable high timber trees, masts for ships of 400 tun: and at the bottom of every hill, a little run of fresh water; but the furthest and last we passed, ranne with a great streame able to drive a mill.[39]

In these raptures Waymouth was concerned not only with the immediate economic potential but also the habitability of the area.

The reports from a tour upstream continued the praise which was bestowed on the area.

From ech banke of this river are divers branching streames into the maine, whereby is affoorded an unspeakable profit by the conveniency of transportation from place to place . . . heere we saw great store of fish, some great, leaping above water, which we judged to be Salmons. All long is an excellent mould of ground. The wood in most places, especially on the East side, very thinne, chiefly oke and some small young birch, bordering low upon the river; all fit for medow and pasture ground: and in that space we went, we had on both sides the river many plaine plots of medow, some of three or foure acres, some eight or nine: so as we judged in the whole to be betweene thirty and forty acres of good grasse, and where the armes run into the Maine, there likewise went a space of both sides of cleere grasse, how far we know not, in many places we might see paths made to come downe to the watering.[40]

After his glowing assessment of the great river and its land Waymouth's final praise was for the produce of the sea. A short distance from the coast the ship came onto a bank where fish were obtained as rapidly as hooks could be tossed overboard. Rosier concluded that fishermen could ". . . make a more profitable returne from hence than from Newfoundland: the fish being so much greater, better fed, and abundant with traine; of which some they desired, and did bring into England to bestow among their friends, and to testifie the true report."[41]

Waymouth also returned with five kidnapped Indians.[42] They were to be taught English and sent back with future expeditions to facilitate English activities in the unknown land. Three of the captured natives were given to Sir Ferdinando Gorges' partner in the first English attempt to colonize on the mainland of New England.[43]

---

[39] Ibid., p. 65.

[40] Ibid., p. 67.

[41] Ibid., p. 71.

[42] Ibid., pp. 59, 75.

[43] Burrage, The Beginnings, p. 44; Gorges in Baxter, op. cit., Vol. II, p. 8; Preston, op. cit., pp. 138-39. Those captives were the Indians incorrectly reported to Champlain as killed by the English.

The glowing report of Waymouth was an important addition to the North American data which were accumulating in England. Within a year of his return various men who had been involved in North American exploration and commerce petitioned for and received from James I letters patent establishing merchant companies to conduct and monopolize future English activities in North America. The patent, issued on April 10, 1606, created two companies for that end. One called in the patent the "first company" is better known as the London or Virginia company. It consisted primarily of Londoners and was assigned rights to territory as far north as 41° N. The "second company" is usually called the Plymouth company because its dominant members were West Countrymen. It was given territory as far south as 38° N, but to avoid conflicts there was to be a one hundred miles distance between the settlements of the two companies. Activity then would determine the effective limits of each company's grant. [44]

The principal protagonists of the second company were Sir John Popham, the Lord Chief Justice of England, and Sir Ferdinando Gorges, who was commencing his long and frustrating role in New England history. Both of them might have been reacting to colonial schemes advanced by Lord Zouche and Waymouth. [45] Popham, in 1606, sent two ships to reconnoiter the New England coast again and to determine its feasibility for a colony. The one commanded by Captain Challons was captured by the Spanish and never reached New England. [46] The other captained by Thomas Hanham with Martin Pring again on board, but as a navigator, successfully accomplished its mission. Although its records have been lost, its report was positive enough to encourage Popham and Gorges to send a colonial

---

[44] Andrews, C. M., The Colonial Period of American History (New Haven: Yale University Press, 1934), Vol. I, pp. 82-83; Brown, Alexander, The Genesis of the United States (New York: Russell & Russell, 1964), Vol. I, pp. 46-64; Calendar of State Papers, Colonial Series (London: H. M. Stationery Office, 1860), Vol. I, pp. 5-6; Howe, op. cit., pp. 147-48; Notestein, Wallace, The English People on the Eve of Colonization 1603-1630 (New York: Harper & Brothers, 1954), pp. 256-57; Strachey, op. cit., pp. 157-58.

[45] Andrews, op. cit., p. 80.

[46] Andrews, op. cit., p. 90; Brown, op. cit., Vol. I, pp. 127-39; Gorges, Ferdinando, A Briefe Relation of the Discovery and Plantation of New England in Baxter, op. cit., Vol. I, pp. 204-5; Purchas, op. cit., Vol. XIX, pp. 269-84.

expedition to the Maine coast the following year.[47]

Under the sponsorship of Popham and Gorges two ships were dispatched to colonize on the Maine coast. In early August, 1607, they arrived at the island which Waymouth had used as his base.[48] Enroute the crew had caught numerous cod and experienced the ". . . aboundaunce of Fish very lardge and great . . . " and ". . . found great stoare of fish all alongst the coast."[49] From St. George's Island the two captains, George Popham and Raleigh Gilbert, sought the Sagadahoc, now the Kennebec River, which had been selected as the general locale for the colony before the expedition left England on the bases of the data returned by Hanham and Pring. However, if Waymouth's great river was the Kennebec rather than the St. George's River, his report could also have been a determining influence; on the other hand his role in a competitive colonial scheme might have promoted rejection of his great river in favor of another stream.

> Capt. Popham, in his pynnace with 30 persons and Captaine Gilbert in his long boat with 18 persons more went early in the morning from their Ship into the Riuer of Sachadehoc to view the River and to search where they might fynd a fitt place for their plantation: they sayled vp into the River nere 14 leagues and found yt to be a very gallant River, very deep and of a good breadth, and full of Fish leaping aboue the water, and seldome lesse water than 3 fathom when they found least: wherevpon they proceeded no farther, but in their returne home-wards they observed manie goodly Islandes therein, and manie braunches of other smale Rivers falling into yt.

The following day the party ". . . went on shoare, and there made choyse of a place for their plantation, at the mouth or entrie of the River on the west-syde, (for, the River bendeth yt self towards the North-east, and Nor-east and by east) being almost an Island of a good bignes. . . . "[50] That site was probably Popham Point, although several alternative places at the Kennebec's mouth are possible.[51] A fort containing houses and a storehouse was con-

---

[47]Andrews, op. cit., p. 91; Gorges, loc. cit.; "Relation of a Voyage to Sagadahoc 1607-1608" in Burrage, Gorges and the Grant, p. 88; Strachey, op. cit., pp. 158-59.

[48]Burrage, Gorges and the Grant, pp. 85, 87; Strachey, op. cit., pp. 164-65.

[49]Strachey, op. cit., pp. 160-61.

[50]Burrage, Gorges and the Grant, pp. 89-90; Strachey, op. cit., p. 167.

[51]Thayer, H. O. (ed.), The Sagadahoc Colony (Portland: Gorges Society, 1892), pp. 167-87, for discussion of the possible sites of this fort.

structed there (Figure 15).[52]

George Popham, one of the colony's leaders, revealed much misinformation about the area's geography. In a letter to James I, sent from "Fort of St. George in Sagadahoc of Virginia," he related that Indians had told him of a large sea seven days journey away. "This cannot be any other than the Southern ocean, reaching to the regions of China, which unquestionably cannot be far from these regions." Further confusion of a nearly mythical character was found in a list of the area's commercial products. "So far as relates to Commerce, there are in these parts, shagbarks, nutmegs, and cinnamon, besides pine wood, and Brazilian cochineal and ambergris, with many other products of great value, and these in greatest aboundance."[53] Nothing as unrealistic as those claims appeared in the other literature of the colony. One can but wonder if Popham was being simply a promoter or had lapsed into Elizabethan fantasies of spices and the riches of the Orient as his death approached.

Exploring parties were sent out and returned with favorable impressions. The islands of Casco Bay were "goodly and gallant," well wooded, but alas like the rest of the area devoid of sassafras. An expedition up the Kennebec yielded the verdict that it was ". . . a Champion land, and very firtile . . . ,"[54] based partially on the sight of many grape vines near present-day Augusta. There an incident with the natives indicated that they were astute observers of the intruders and had more contact with them than the surviving records tell. The natives noticed that fire was necessary for the

---

[52] A plan of this fort was found in the Simancas Archives and reproduced in Brown, op. cit., Vol. I, pp. 190-94. Certain aspects of the drawing suggest that it was not an eyewitness sketch but rather one perhaps made from interviews because it contained stylized features typical of European forts of the period which could not have been done in the brief time available to the builders. The walls of the fort appear to be stone. The Davies narrative nowhere indicated stone as the building material. A log palisade would be a more reasonable type. Architectural embellishments such as the cupolas on the land gate probably would not have been made under the circumstances. See Shurtleff, H. R., The Log Cabin Myth (Cambridge: Harvard University Press, 1939), pp. 74-76, for a differing interpretation.

[53] Thayer, op. cit., p. 119. Popham was perhaps told of the St. Lawrence-Great Lakes but interpreted the information within the framework of the search for the Northwest Passage. See Brown, op. cit., Vol. I, pp. 145-46.

[54] Strachey, op. cit., pp. 168-69.

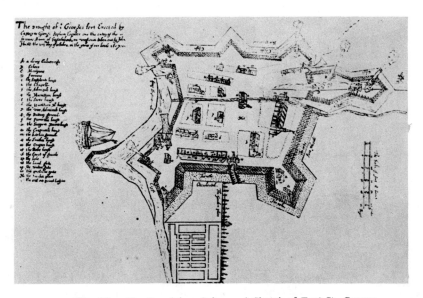

Fig. 15.--The Sagadahoc Colony: A Sketch of Fort St. George

English muskets to shoot. To protect his people from English guns,
one native seized the only brand among the English and tossed it
into the river. The general assessment of the Kennebec area was
that ". . . they found aboundaunce of Spruse Trees such as are
able to maast the greatest shipp his Maiestie hath, and many other
trees, oake, walnut, Pineapple: Fish aboundaunce: great store of
Grapes, hoppes, and Chiballs, also they found certayne Codes in
which they supposed, the cotton wooil to grow; and also vpon the
Banckes many shells of pearle."[55]

Something of those impressions reached Gorges who wrote to
Robert Cecil, the King's secretary, two weeks before Popham's
antiquated letter to the king.

> . . . With great newes of a fertill Contry, gallant Rivers, stately Harbors, and a
> people tractable . . . but no returne to satisfy the expectation of the Adventurers, the
> wch may bee an occasion, to blemish the reputacion of the designe, although in reason
> it could not bee otherwayes, both bycause of the shortness of theyr aboad there (wch
> was but two monethes) as also, theyr want of meanes to follow theyr directions, theyr
> number being so small, and theyr business so great, beside in very truthe, the defect
> and wante of understandinge of some of those imployed, to performe what they weare
> directed unto . . . there will bee divers reasons to perswade a constant resolution to
> persue this place, as firste the bouldnes of the Coaste, the easines of the navigation,
> the fertility of the soyle, and the severall sortes of Commodityes, that they ar ashured,
> the contry do yealde, as namely fish in the season, in great plenty, all the Coste
> alonge mastidge for shipps, goodly oakes, and Ceaders, wth infint other sortes of
> trees, Rason, hempe, grapes very fayre and excellent good, wherof they have already
> made wine, much like to the Claret wine that comes out of France, rich furrs if they
> can keepe the Frenchmen from the trade, as for mettalls they can say nothinge, but
> they ar confidente there is in the Contry, if they had meanes to seeke for it, neither
> could they go so high, as the Allom mines are, wch the Savages doth ashure them
> there is great plenty of.[56]

The principal contribution of the Popham colony to the image
of New England was its failure which truncated the developing
image of an abundant land whose exploitation would be facilitated
by English colonization. Instead it became the basis of an image
in which it was doubtful that the area could permanently be inhabited by the English. The colony was abandoned in the late summer
of 1608 when the surviving men returned to England. Conditions in
the colony had some parallel to those in the early years of Jamestown which fortunately for the future of English colonization did
not have a comparable finis. In the Sagadahoc colony leadership
was divided between the elderly Popham and the younger Gilbert.[57]

---

[55] Ibid., pp. 170-71.

[56] Thayer, op. cit., pp. 132-33.

[57] See Preston, op. cit., p. 146, for an evaluation of these men as leaders.

Because of Popham's death during the winter and Gilbert's immi-
nent departure to assume the Gilbert estates, the colony on the
eve of its abandonment faced the prospect of being leaderless,
which in fact it might have been during the winter--or at least vic-
timized by ineffectual leadership. Difficulties of other sorts than
divided leadership plagued the colony. Many of the men evidently
refused to do their assigned tasks or to cooperate with others for
their common good, and dissensions arose between the quarreling
groups. [58] Also the colonists were constantly fearful of attacks by
the French or by the Indians. [59]

Because of the divided, ineffectual leadership, internal dis-
organization, and inadequate preparations the colony suffered hard-
ships during the winter. Ill-prepared and ineffectually governed,
the colony's misfortunes worsened when the storehouse and some
of the sleeping quarters burned. [60] Few details on the specific
nature of the winter have survived so that it is impossible to com-
pare it with the miserable one suffered by de Monts and his men.
The Davies-Strachey narrative made only brief mention of the winter and tried to mitigate it by the observation that the same winter
in Europe was extremely severe. "Many discoveries likewise had
bene made both to the Mayne and vnto the neigh-bour-Ryvers, and
the Frontier-Nations fully discovered by the diligence of Capt.
Gilbert had not the winter proved so extreame vnseasonable and
frostie for yt being in the yeare 1607 when the extraordinary Frost
was felt in most partes of Europe, yt was here likewise as vehe-
ment, by which no boat could stirre vpon busines. . . ."[61] The
English were having their first experience with the cold, snow,
and frozen waters of a New England winter. An excerpt from a
sailor's testimony in Admiralty Court records reveals a small

---

[58] In England the death of Sir John Popham had deprived the colony of an important sponsor. Baxter, op. cit., Vol. II, pp. 16-17; Burrage, Gorges and the Grant, p. 93; Strachey, op. cit., p. 173; and Sir William Alexander, pp. 193-94.

[59] Banks, C. E., "New Documents Relating to the Popham Expedition, 1607," Proceedings of the American Antiquarian Society, New Series, XXXIX (October, 1929), 311; Preston, op. cit., p. 147.

[60] Baxter, op. cit., Vol. I, p. 206.

[61] Burrage, Gorges and the Grant, p. 98; Strachey, op. cit., p. 173.

episode, ". . . that the Wentar was verey foule & the Ice greate
while the said shipp remayned in the harbour of Sakadahoc in the
north pts of Virginia. . . ."[62] The ship in question had planks
broken by the pressure of the ice. Gorges informed Cecil that
". . . the extremity of the winter, hath ben great, and hath sorely
pinched our People. . . ."[63] Among the lost evidence on the happenings of the winter were the journals of Gilbert which contained
the opinion of the harsh winter as the cause of abandonment, probably the easiest explanation which Gilbert's pride allowed.[64]

However much the winter's severity might have caused the
colony's abandonment, the contemporary mind associated the two
in cause and effect. ". . . The Country it selfe was branded by
the returne of the Plantation, as being over cold, and in respect
of that, not habitable by our Nation."[65] From that association
arose the image of New England as uninhabitable, a situation which
precluded any permanent settlement there for many years. Schemes
to establish a permanent base of operations for English adventures
in New England were discontinued, while Jamestown, the colony of
the first company, continued its tenuous existence. "The arriuall
of these people heere in England, was wonderfull discouragement
to all the first vndertakers, in so much as there was no more
speech of setling any other plantation in those parts for a long
time after. . . ."[66] A mid-eighteenth century account summed up
the image of New England in the aftermath of the Popham colony
failure. "And thus was this Plantation begun and ended in one
Year; and that vast Grant, in which lay large Tracts of fine and
Noble Country, was stigmatized in the Gross, and despised, as
cold, barren, mountainous and rocky Desert."[67]

---

[62]Banks, op. cit., pp. 318, 321, 324, 327, 330, 334.

[63]Thayer, op. cit., p. 137.

[64]Brown, op. cit., Vol. I, p. 197; Thayer, op. cit., p. 89.

[65]Baxter, op. cit., Vol. II, p. 17.

[66]Baxter, op. cit., Vol. I, p. 207; Preston, op. cit., p. 149.

[67]Stith, op. cit., p. 75. See also Prince, Thomas, A Chronological History of New England (Boston: Kneeland and Green, 1736), Vol. II, p. 38.

The area's promise of wealth was not totally ignored, however, although the experience of the Popham colony seemed to rule
out resident exploitation. Sir Francis Popham, heir of the colony's
principal sponsor, continued the commercial pattern of Gosnold,
Pring, and Waymouth. He periodically sent ships to the coast to
fish and collect furs.[68] In 1614 John Smith found one of Popham's
ships at anchor by the mainland near Monhegan Island. The captain of that ship had been there so often and was so well known to
the Indians that he dominated the regional fur trade.[69] Gorges
after a brief interest in the Virginia Company continued to be
active in the occasional trade to the New England coast so ". . .
when God should be pleased, by our ordinary frequenting that Country, to make it appear that it would yield both profit and content.
. . ."[70] By 1614 Gorges was again solely involved with New
England and sponsored vessels which were not only commercial but
also explored. His agent, Richard Vines, wintered at the mouth of
the Saco River in 1616-17 expressly to ascertain if Englishmen
could survive the rigors of a New England winter. He did, but no
plantation by Gorges was immediately forthcoming.[71]

In the decade preceding Pilgrim settlement of New England,
fur trade and fishing activities were centered at Monhegan Island,
although Pemiquid and Damariscove (Damerill's Cove) shared both
pursuits.[72] The total extent of those activities and now much the
mainland was involved are unanswered questions. The few isolated
references to ships on the New England coast such as Smith's list
of ten ships between 1614 and 1619 and Hawkins' visit in 1615 with
two ships add up to a small percentage of the contemporary traffic

---

[68]Andrews, op. cit., Vol. I, p. 95; Banks, op. cit., p. 314; Baxter, op. cit., Vol. I,
p. 207; Gilman, op. cit., p. 29.

[69]Arber, E. (ed.), Travels and Works of Captain John Smith (Edinburgh: John Grant,
1910), Vol. I, p. 188.

[70]Baxter, op. cit., Vol. II, p. 18. Immediately after the failure of the Sagadahoc
colony Gorges became active for the Virginia Company for seven years after which he
returned to promotion of New England. See Preston, op. cit., p. 150.

[71]Baxter, op. cit., Vol. II, pp. 18-19.

[72]Bolton, C. K., The Real Founders of New England (Boston: F. W. Faxon, 1929),
pp. 111-12, 167, 170-72.

to the Newfoundland fishery.[73] Addition of vessels assumed to
have been sent by Popham, Gorges, and others does not yield a significant increase in the total. These data led Gorges' biographer
to conclude that the New England coast and its fisheries were not
widely used by the English. Other scholars have interpreted this
evidence to indicate active English fishing and trading, establishment of trading stations, and possible wintering by fishermen.[74]

During this period the Virginia colony used the New England
fisheries. The same Captain Argall who was later to rout the
French from the Maine coast reached Cape Cod in 1610 and sailed
on to the mouth of the Kennebec after he had been driven off course
on a voyage to Bermuda. While on the New England coast his crew
was put to fishing, and the vessel returned to Jamestown with a
cargo of fish.[75] The voyage during which he attacked the French
might have been a routine fishing one.[76] Hawkins sailed to Virginia in 1615 with a cargo of fish for that colony. Father Biard
claimed that the Virginians were making annual summer visits to
the coast to get cod for the winter.[77] At the end of the decade
fishing by Virginians was so frequent that the New England Council
complained to the Privy Council about their encroachments into its
territory.[78] Because the records do not mention furs or timber,
it is assumed that the Virginians were interested only in the
fisheries.

The last decade before settlement of the coast witnessed the
arrival into New England history of one of the most dynamic, color-
ful, and controversial figures of English exploration in North

---

[73]Arber, op. cit., Vol. I, pp. 241-42; Barbour, Philip L., The Three Worlds of
Captain John Smith (London: Macmillan, 1964), pp. 332-33; Lounsbury, R. G., The British Fishery at Newfoundland 1634-1763 (New Haven: Yale University Press, 1934), pp. 33ff.

[74]Andrews, op. cit., pp. 94-95; Brown, op. cit., Vol. II, pp. 779-80; Preston, op.
cit., p. 153.

[75]Levermore, op. cit., Vol. II, pp. 428-37; Percy, George, "A Trewe Relacyon,"
Tyler's Quarterly, III (1922), 270-71.

[76]See Chapter III, p. 87.

[77]Levermore, op. cit., Vol. II, p. 491; Preston, op. cit., p. 158.

[78]"Records of the New England Company," Proceedings of the American Antiquarian
Society, XLVII (April, 1867), 78.

America, Captain John Smith. His brief visit to the coast was related to several trends which were working to renew interest in the area. Seven years had passed since the failure of the Popham colony, and the immediate reaction to it was dissipated by time. The commercial voyages of the younger Popham, Gorges, and others by demonstrating the validity of the area's commercial prospects helped to restore its reputation from total discredit. Gorges' interest in establishing a New England base had revived but was refocused southward of the Kennebec. The precarious but tenacious existence of Jamestown proved to those who were doubtful about American colonization in general that an English colony could survive in North America, and the fishermen communities of Newfoundland provided more evidence of habitability. Newfoundland was also a factor because its increasingly successful fisheries caused English groups excluded from the profit to seek an area capable of rivaling it. French and Dutch voyages along the coast made the English aware of their potential exclusion from it or loss of it if stronger controls were not instituted. For Smith himself personal considerations included a desire to redeem the tarnished reputation with which he had returned from Virginia and a zeal to develop a colony which would rival Virginia and repay the London Company for its lack of gratitude to him for saving its colony.[79]

The expedition which Smith commanded in the summer of 1614 was a traditional combination of commerce and exploration. The commercial phase of his voyage was a disappointment, if not a downright failure. He was sent to get whales and whale oil--in itself a strange task for that complex man, but as the beasts were elusive he attempted to catch a cargo of fish off Monhegan Island. He arrived after the best fishing season. Although some fish were taken, the amount was neither impressive nor valuable. French traders and an agent of Popham had obtained the choice furs before his arrival. He ignored the order to search for gold. Instead he

---

[79]For differing interpretations of Smith consult Barbour, op. cit.; Rozwenc, Edwin C., "Captain John Smith's Image of America," William and Mary Quarterly, 3rd Series, XVI (January, 1959), 27-36; Taylor, Late Tudor . . . , p. 162; Willison, George F., Behold Virginia! the Fifth Crown (New York: Harcourt, Brace and Company, 1952). For evidence of Dutch activities see O'Callaghan, E. B. (ed.), Documents Relative to the Colonial History of the State of New York (Albany: Weed, Parsons and Company, 1856), Vol. I, pp. 10-14.

explored the coast.[80]

Smith ranged from the Penobscot to the northern part of Cape Cod.[81] None of this coast was completely unknown or unexplored by the English, but Smith entered many sections bypassed by his predecessors and surveyed the area as a unit, a task which only Champlain before him had done. Hence his work had details and a sense of totality and continuity absent from earlier English reports. Importantly for his relation to later developments his ideas about New England were incorporated into books written during his propagandist period which dated from his return to England until his death in 1631 and onto his map of New England.[82] With the circulation of those tracts, his name became associated with the cause of English settlement in New England, although his actual experience in the area was limited to three months. He also bestowed the name by which the area was to be known in modern times, New England, giving it an individual identity which it lacked as long as it was known as the north of Virginia. Posterity used his name for the region, but most of the other place names which he applied on his map never gained popular favor.

Smith's analysis differentiated New England into northern and southern parts. His descriptions of northern New England repeated many characteristics which had been observed earlier. He noted the many good harbors, the numerous off-shore islands, the vast forests, the many rivers, the abundance of fish and fowl, and a small Indian population.[83] But he was a more critical evaluator than his predecessors had been. For example, contrast his assessment of the Kennebec with the florid prose of Rosier or Davies.

---

[80]Arber, op. cit., Vol. I, pp. 187-88; Barbour, op. cit., pp. 306-8.

[81]Arber, op. cit., Vol. I, p. 192; Barbour, op. cit., p. 308.

[82]Smith's Description of New England was first published in 1616. New Englands Trials appeared in 1620, a second edition in 1622. In slightly altered form those materials were included as the sixth book of his Generall Histories of Virginia, New England, & the Summer Isles (1624) wherein data of the Pilgrim settlement were included. Appropriately his final promotion in 1631 was Advertisement for the Unexperienced Planters of New England, or Any Where. The map of New England was printed in 1616. See Chapter I of this study for a discussion of it and Brown, op. cit., Vol. II, p. 780, for the opinion that it might not be based on Smith's survey.

[83]Arber, op. cit., Vol. I, p. 237.

"Along this Riuer 40 or 50 miles, I saw nothing but great high cliffs of barren Rocks, ouergrowne with wood: but where the Saluages dwelt, the ground is exceeding fat and fertill." Of the coast west of the Penobscot which had also been rapturously described he wrote,

> But all this Coast to <u>Pennobscot,</u> and as farre I could see Eastward of it, is nothing but such high craggy Cliffy Rocks and stony Illes that I wondered such great trees could growe vpon so hard foundations. It is a Countrie rather to affright, then delight one. And how to describe a more plaine spectacle of desolation, or more barren, I knowe not. Yet the Sea there is the strangest fishpond I euer saw; and those barren Iles so furnished with good woods, springs, fruits, fish, and foule, that it makes mee thinke, though the Coast be rockie, and thus affrightable; the Vallies, Plaines, and interior parts may well . . . be very fertile. . . .[84]

Smith had seen too much of North America to think the Maine portion as its most preferable.

In his evaluation of the southern part of New England as better than the northern sector he reflected both his ability to put things into a judgment which stood the test of time and his knowledge that potential English backers of a colony such as Gorges were then interested in the southern, not northern part of the coast. If he was partially directed in his judgments, he also made assessments of the area biased to his own personal desire to found a colony. Because of that bias he put a premium on agriculture as evidence of a hospitable and habitable land. "Here is ground also as good as any lyeth in the height of forty one, forty two, forty three, &, which is as temperate and as fruitfull as any other parallel in the world."[85] He followed that statement with the standard argument of his times, a recitation of the productive areas of Europe found at those latitudes.

He considered the coast around Massachusetts Bay superior to anything seen in Maine. In that judgment his desire to find a satisfactory colonial location made him particularly responsive to an area where Indian agriculture was most evident.

> And then the Countrie of the <u>Massachusets</u>, which is the Paradise of all those parts. For, heere are many Iles all planted with corne; groues, mulberries, saluage gardens, and good harbours: the Coast is for the most part, high clayie sandie cliffs. The Sea Coast as you passe, shewes you all along large corne fields, and great troupes of well proportioned people: but the <u>French</u> hauing remained heere neere six weekes, left

---

[84] <u>Ibid.</u>, Vol. I, pp. 203-4.

[85] <u>Ibid.</u>, Vol. I, p. 196; Taylor, <u>Late Tudor and Early Stuart</u>, p. 162.

nothing for vs to take occasion to examine the inhabitants relations, viz. if there be near three thousand people vpon these Iles, and that the River doth pearce many daies iourneies the intralles of that Countrey.[86]

He did not consider the natives to be a deterrent factor. "We found the people in those parts verie kinde; but in their furie no lesse valiant." He did think them inferior and unable to realize the promise of the land. "Then come you to Accomack, an excellent good harbor, good land; and no want of any thing but industrious people." To him Cape Cod was ". . . onley a headland of high hills of sand ouergrowne with shrubble pines, hurts, and such trash; but an excellent harbor for all weathers." He was more honest than one might expect of a promoter about the nature of the outer Cape waters. "Towards the South and Southwest of this Cape, is found a long and dangerous shoale of sands and rocks." Importantly he warned that the fur trade would not flourish on the southern coast because ". . . the furs Northward are much better, and in much more plentie, then Southward."[87]

Smith realized that achievement of his long term goal of a flourishing colony depended on participation sustained by immediate profit. Sensible enough not to base his case on rumors of undiscovered precious metals, he stressed the commodity which was returning a profit--fish.[88] His argument that New England fishing began earlier than in Newfoundland so that New England fish would be first on the market was borrowed from earlier commentators, who also started the comparable claim that New England was a more satisfactory base of fishing operations. Smith detailed the markets--Canary Islands, Spain, Portugal, Provence, Savoy, Sicily, Italy, Norway, Sweden, and Germany--and pointed out the value of exchange cargoes of pitch, tar, wines, oils, sugars, and silks as well as the increased employment of ships and men.[89]

In his search for colonial supporters among merchants involved in the fish trade, Smith used the comparison to Newfoundland's profit as an enticement, but merchants familiar with developments in the Newfoundland situation would have been aware of conditions which Smith ignored but which would have lessened

---

[86] Arber, op. cit., Vol. I, pp. 204-5.

[87] Ibid., Vol. I, pp. 205-6.

[88] Ibid., Vol. I, p. 194.

[89] Ibid., Vol. I, pp. 239-40.

enthusiasm to support a scheme combining colony and fishing. Settlement in Newfoundland led immediately to quarrels between fishermen and colonists. The two groups contested rather than complemented each other. ". . . Each group strove to control the fishery and to oust the other, bequeathing to future generations of planters and fishermen a heritage of hatred, violence, and mutual jealousy."[90] Perhaps with the Newfoundland experience as precedence for the idea of incompatibility of fishing and settlement, West Country groups active in the Plymouth Company opposed colonization where it would compete with their commercial fishing.[91]

Like his vision of the Massachusetts lands settled by an industrious people, the fishing trade which Smith prophesied would be realized by others at a later time without direct influence from him. His role was not to effect action but to alter the image within which the action--settlement in this case--would be accomplished. He restored habitability to the popular image of New England and returned the image status to what it had been following Waymouth's voyage. But unable to establish a colony, Smith could offer no proof of habitability. That evidence was supplied by the Pilgrim experience, the importance of which Smith fully realized.[92]

---

[90] Lounsbury, op. cit., p. 39.

[91] Taylor, Late Tudor and Early Stuart, p. 161.

[92] At one time Smith tried to associate himself with the Pilgrims, but there is no evidence other than his words of that action. Purchas was another of the few Englishmen of the period who sensed the long term importance of the Pilgrim settlement and included materials on it in his collection. See Purchas, op. cit., Vol. XIX, pp. 312-94.

CHAPTER V

AS THE HOME OF ENGLISHMEN

Overseas settlement as it was conceived during late Elizabethan and early Stuart times was viewed as an adjunct of economic
exploitation. Proponents of colonization argued that a colony
would ensure English control over an area worthy of exploitation
and systematic collection of goods desired in England. Within that
conception the primary function of an overseas colony was to provide supportive services for English economic and political advancement. Before such a colony could be established, it was necessary
to justify the expenditure of money by showing that a profit could
be extracted from the area's commodities and to make some judgment of the area's habitability. As reports of expeditions illustrated, the only tangible bases for the latter were short visits in
fall or summer months during which the evidence of native agriculture, familiar vegetation, and brief experiments of planting European crops was collected.

Before 1620 only one English settlement is known to have
been undertaken on the New England coast within that conception of
operations. The Sagadahoc or Popham colony was abandoned under
circumstances which developed an image that all or most of the
coast was uninhabitable either in the short or long term. The continuing and increasing collection of furs and fish further demonstrated to some minds the validity of the arguments that a colony
was supportive but not necessitous to such activities. That theo-
retical position on colonies together with the dismal experience of
the Popham venture made colonial sponsorship a questionable and
dubious task.

After 1615 the reputation of the New England coast as inhospitable and uninhabitable slowly altered, but not to the point of
attracting ready sponsors for a colony there. The examples of
occasional fishing stations along the northern coast and of Gorges'

agents, Vines and Dermer, to the south, provided evidence that Englishmen could live and survive--at least on a short term basis-- in New England. Those examples did little to advance the cause of colonization beyond the pre-1607 situation which Smith restored-- that a colony to support and sustain the collection of furs and fish was feasible. While Smith was forced by practical considerations to link his scheme of New England colonization with commercial activities, his promotion ended in an image of the region as the permanent home of Englishmen. His detachment from the earlier economic image is best seen in his vision of the Massachusetts Bay region being civilized by his countrymen. Economically he had depicted the bay area as less favorable for fish and furs than the northern sector but had proclaimed it the more suitable for settle- ment because he saw there the potential to sustain a new England, not just an economic outpost of empire. Gorges in his shift of focus from northern to southern New England might have implicitly changed to the new image--indeed possibly be part of the inspira- tion for Smith's ideas, but Gorges' ultimate failure to be either an effective exploiter of resources or an effective promoter of settle- ment lay in his persistent commitment to Elizabethan procedures and in his inability to understand or adapt to new forces which would dominate New England settlement in the first half of the seventeenth century.[1] At least by June, 1620, his agent, Thomas Dermer, shared part of Smith's vision for the Bay region.[2] By 1620 it was apparent that the image of New England as an area of settlement required more than commercial motivation if it was to compete with or replace the image of the region simply as an area of economic exploitation. The realization of the settlement image, however, was to be more a matter of accident than purposive intent and achieved by people with no prior contacts with the coast rather than by persons involved before 1620.

The new settlement image of the area as one suitable for per- manent habitation by Englishmen contained features of the older

---

[1]Pomfret, John E., *Founding the American Colonies 1583-1660* (New York: Harper & Row, 1970), pp. 146-47.

[2]Bradford, William, *History of Plymouth Plantation 1620-1647* (Boston: Massachu- setts Historical Society, 1912), Vol. I, pp. 206-7.

exploitive one. Both fish and furs were important aspects of later economic relationships of the Pilgrims and the Puritans with England, other countries of western Europe, and the West Indies. Fish became one of the staples of colonial New England trade, while the settlers' assessment of the area's fur potential was to prove less perceptive than that made by the French in the early years of the seventeenth century.[3] The retention of fish and fur exploitation as practical but not dominant features in the settlement image illustrated the progression of image development. The fish and furs were components which could be traced back to Elizabethan times, but the dominant aspects of the new image arose from the contemporary problems of early Stuart England.

New motivation as well as proof that the new image was realistic and achievable came from the religious disputes of the era. The Pilgrims, a separatist group dissatisfied with foreign exile and unwilling to return to persecution in England, decided to emigrate from Holland to North America. Their agents in England approached the Virginia Company rather than Gorges or the Plymouth Company to obtain the privilege of settling within its grant.[4] After difficult and sometimes confused negotiations the company did grant a patent, but it did not specify where in the company's lands the Pilgrims were to settle, although it is assumed that they were expected to land somewhere near the mouth of the Hudson River.[5]

---

[3] Buffinton, A. H., "New England and the Western Fur Trade, 1629-1675, " Publications of the Colonial Society of Massachusetts, XVIII (1915-1916), 160-63.

[4] It is impossible from the surviving evidence to determine why the Pilgrims went to the Virginia Company. It is here assumed that the considerations were the success of the Jamestown colony in creating a favorable image for the Virginia Company lands, the almost inactive state of the Plymouth Company, and the access of the Pilgrims' agents to contacts in London. See Morison, Samuel E. (ed.), Of Plymouth Plantation 1620-1647 (New York: Random House-Modern Library, 1952), p. 29, for his explanation.

[5] Andrews, C. M., The Colonial Period of American History (New Haven: Yale University Press, 1934), Vol. I, pp. 249ff.; Langdon, G. D., Plymouth Colony: A History of New Plymouth 1620-1691 (New Haven: Yale University Press, 1966), p. 2; Maverick, Samuel, "A Briefe Discription of New England and the Severall Townes Therein, " Proceedings of the Massachusetts Historical Society, 2nd Series, I (October, 1884), 242; Morton, Nathaniel, New-Englands Memoriall (Boston: Club of Odd Volumes, 1903 [reprint of 1669 edition]), pp. 5, 12; Pory, John, John Pory's Lost Description of Plymouth Colony (Boston: Houghton Mifflin, 1918), pp. 35-36; Prince, Thomas, A Chronological History of New England (Boston: Kneeland and Green, 1736), Vol. III, p. 8. For the Pilgrim version of the negotiations see Bradford, op. cit., Vol. I, pp. 65, 70ff., 99ff.

The cause of the Pilgrim arrival at Cape Cod is disputed.
The thesis that it was a Dutch plot to divert the English settlers
from the area of Dutch claims is now discredited.[6] The contention
that a purposive decision was made to settle north of the Virginia
patent limits before they left England has its proponents.[7] However, it is difficult to reconcile either of these interpretations
with the explanation of the Pilgrims. Their ship, off course,
sighted the continent at a higher latitude than originally intended.
After vain and nearly disastrous attempts to pass through the
Cape's shoally waters to return to a lower latitude, they determined because of the lateness of the season (November) and shortage of supplies to establish themselves at a satisfactory site close
at hand.[8]

The accidental interpretation of the Pilgrims' arrival in
southern New England means that any information which might have
been collected about any originally projected settlement area within
the Virginia patent was of little or no value in the selection of a
site along the shores of Cape Cod, that they probably knew little,
if anything, of the character of the region where they found themselves, and that they were acting independently of the influences
and factors which altered the coast's image after the Popham colony
failure. The latter two theses are suggested by the absence of references to their predecessors on the coast from the older of the
two principal sources on Pilgrim settlement, the inclusion of such
references in the later Bradford work, and the surveys which were
made before the Plymouth site was chosen.[9] Hence in the process

---

[6]Bradford, op. cit., Vol. I, pp. 158-61; Morton, op. cit., p. 12; Young, Alexander
(ed.), Chronicles of the First Planters of the Colony of Massachusetts Bay (Boston:
Charles C. Little and James Brown, 1846), p. 4; Young, Alexander (ed.), Chronicles of
the Pilgrim Fathers (Boston: Charles C. Little and James Brown, 1841), p. 101.

[7]Coleman, R. V., The First Frontier (New York: Charles Scribner's Sons, 1948),
p. 128; Mather, Cotton, Magnalia Christi Americana (Hartford: Silas Andrus and Son,
1855), Vol. I, p. 49.

[8]Bradford, op. cit., Vol. I, pp. 152-62; Parry, J. H., The Age of Reconnaissance
(London: Weidenfeld and Nicolson, 1963), p. 218. A practical discussion of the naviga-
tional problems involved in the decision may be found in Nickerson, W. S., Land Ho!--
1620: A Seaman's Story of the Mayflower (Boston: Houghton, Mifflin, 1931).

[9]The earlier volume, Mourt's Relation, was published in 1622 and partially reprinted
in Purchas' collection of 1624, while Bradford's history was not begun until 1630 and was

by which the Pilgrims determined on the Plymouth site we have the first evaluation of any New England area as a permanent overseas home of Englishmen on the basis of its ability to sustain a resident population rather than the presence of exploitable commodities.

The Pilgrim involvement with the image of New England as a habitable area had three phases. The first concerned the general habitability of the North American regions claimed by England and available for settlement. That phase was conducted before they left Holland and concluded in a positive verdict in so far as the northern lands of the Virginia Company were assessed. It possibly might also have been applied to the southern part of New England because of the vagueness and imprecision with which regional names were then used. A mid and late seventeenth century definition of "New England" which included the coasts of New Jersey and New York, the area which was the northern sector of the Virginia Company patent, is one indication that contemporary conceptions about the various parts of the Atlantic coast should not be confined to present-day regional boundaries.[10] It is conceivable that the habitable image of the northern sector of the Virginia Company patent was vaguely applied to the southern portion of Smith's New England which, if his map be the guide, had its southern border at Cape Cod. The confusion on regional definition is further illustrated by the term "north part of Virginia," as used in the Mayflower Compact. There the phrase could have been either the pre-Smith regional designation for New England or reference to a presumed location within the limits of the Virginia Company patent.[11]

---

completed about 1650. See Bradford, op. cit., Vol. I, pp. xv-xvi, and Purchas, Samuel, Hakluytus Posthumus or Purchas His Pilgrimes (New York: AMS Press, 1965), Vol. XIX, pp. 312-43. Comparable interpretation of the Pilgrims' knowledge on arrival may be found in Rutman, Darrett B., "The Pilgrims and Their Harbor," William and Mary Quarterly, 3rd Series, XVII (April, 1960), 164-75.

[10] Josselyn, John, New Englands Rarities (London: G. Widdowes, 1672), in Archaeologia Americana, IV (1860), 138; Mather, op. cit., Vol. I, p. 45; Morton, op. cit., p. 5.

[11] Josselyn, John, An Account of Two Voyages to New-England (London: G. Widdowes, 1675) in Collections of the Massachusetts Historical Society, 3rd Series, III (1833), 370, 374. An example of the contemporary confusion in the use of terms is the phrase "the Northerne parts of Virginia" which occurs in the Mayflower Compact. It is impossible from context to ascertain if the older place name was used or if the reference was to relative location within the Virginia Company patent. If the latter, then the phrase is evidence that the Pilgrims did not know that they were beyond the northern limit of that patent. See Bradford, op. cit., Vol. I, p. 191.

The second phase was the selection of some part of the shores of Cape Cod Bay as the locale for their colony, and the third phase determined the specific site where they located the structures and functions of their settlement. In contrast to the first phase where the evidence for the bases of Pilgrim decision is lacking, the second and third phases are documented. Mourt's Relation, written two years after the colony was founded, is as close to the activities of the last two phases of landscape perception and evaluation as the modern reader may get. It is a straightforward and detailed account of the first two years of the colony; in it the events culminating in the choice of Plymouth were recorded. [12]

Although the journal told little of their preconceptions--if they had any--or their initial reaction to the region, there was nothing in it to suggest the bleak and harsh vision which Bradford wrote later and read more like a Puritan tract on the wilderness than the promotional characteristics of the journal. Here is Bradford's remembrance of the group's reaction to New England written nearly twenty years after their arrival. [13]

> . . . For the season it was Winter, and they that know the Winters of the Country, know them to be sharp and violent, subject to cruel and fierce Storms, dangerous to travel to known places, much more to search unknown Coasts. Besides, what could they see but a hideous and desolate wilderness, full of wilde Beasts and wilde Men? and what multitudes of them there were, they knew not: neither could they as it were go up to the top of Pisgah, to view from this Wilderness a more goodly Country to feed their hopes; for which way soever they turned their eyes . . . they could have little solace or content in respect of any outward object, for Summer being ended, all things stand in appearance with a weather-beaten face, and the whole Country full of Woods and Thickets, represented a wilde and savage hew; if they looked behinde them, there was the mighty Ocean which they had passed, and was now as a main Bar and Gulph to separate them from all the Civil Parts of the World.

The backgrounds of the people who arrived on the Mayflower are important considerations to get some measure of their ability to judge the area as a homeland and to assess the quality of their judgment. In addition to the ship's crew, the passengers may be divided into three categories. There were the exiled Separatists

---

[12] The version used for this study is Dexter, H. M. (ed.), Mourt's Relation or a Journal of the Plantation at Plymouth (Boston: John K. Wiggin, 1865). A newer edition is Heath, Dwight B. (ed.), A Journal of the Pilgrims at Plymouth (New York: Corinth Books, 1963), but it lacks the valuable notes of the Dexter edition.

[13] Morison (ed.), p. 62. The passage also occurs in Morton, op. cit., p. 13. For a study of the concept of New England as a bleak, forbidding wilderness habitat in Puritan literature, see Carroll, Peter N., Puritanism and the Wilderness (New York: Columbia University Press, 1969).

who had spent some seventeen years in the urban environment of
Leyden, Holland, English Separatists who joined the expedition
shortly before it left England, and non-Separatist workmen who had
been assigned to the expedition by Weston and his associates.
These were all simple folk, but there is no evidence that any of
them had been directly involved in husbandry in the years immediately preceding the departure to the New World. The exiles had
been chiefly printers and clothworkers in Holland, although they
had been village dwellers before their removal to Leyden. The
English contingent who came mostly from London was also primarily artisans. None of the entire party, with the exception of the
ship's captain and some of the crew, had any direct prior contact
with the New World. On the basis of their backgrounds the Pilgrims were not well prepared to assess the general livability of
the coast where they found themselves or to select the best agricultural lands there. But being intelligent persons, they were able to
devise satisfactory, if not the best, criteria to guide their choice.
And fortunately for their long-term survival, the natives taught
them the skills most immediate and most lacking for their subsis-
tence--how to be productive farmers. [14]

The assessment of the region and site selection began when
the _Mayflower_ put into Provincetown harbor and lay at anchor for
five weeks during which the country was explored. The Pilgrim
description of that harbor contains some categories of landscape
features which they observed and assessed in their search for a
settlement site. That anchorage was ". . . a good harbour and
pleasant Bay, circled round, except in the entrance . . . compassed about to the very Sea with Okes, Pines, Iuniper, Sassafras,
and other sweet wood; it is a harbour wherein 1000 saile of Ships
may safely ride. . . . " Whales in the bay indicated to the ship's
master and mate a better whaling ground than Greenland, but the
fishing was disappointing. No cod were seen, and no other ocean
fish were caught during the stay there. The principal drawback
was an inshore depth so shallow that ". . . we could not neere the

---

[14] Fussell, G. E., "Social and Agrarian Background of the Pilgrim Fathers," _Agri-
cultural History_, VIII (1933), 183-202; Rutman, D. B., _Husbandmen of Plymouth_ (Boston:
Beacon Press, 1967), pp. 4-5; Willison, G. F., _Saints and Strangers_ (New York: Reynal
and Hitchcock, 1945), pp. 11-120.

shore by three quarters of an English mile. . . ."[15] The lack of
fresh water also was part of its rejection as the settlement site,
for although Mourt's Relation stated that the ship's water supply
was replenished there, Bradford wrote of a water shortage.[16]
These descriptions as well as others in the journal discount Morton's later claim that the Pilgrims considered the Cape barren,
although Bradford recorded that the people on the second ship
which came to Plymouth thought the Cape ". . . nothing but a
naked and barren place."[17]

From the Provincetown base the Pilgrims conducted three
land and water exploring expeditions, known respectively as the
first, second, or third discovery, to find a satisfactory site for
their settlement. During those expeditions the text of Mourt's
Relation indicates that the observations were concentrated on two
basic categories of landscape features: (1) indigenous land uses
and their sites and (2) natural phenomena which were necessitous
to sustain the English settlers.

Between the visit of Smith when the southern New England
coast was described as populous and the arrival of the Pilgrims
the coastal Indian population had been decimated by plague.[18] Initially the Pilgrims did not seem aware of the altered circumstance,
although in retrospect the small number of Indians was viewed as
an important factor in the early survival of the colony.[19] Not
until Squanto's coming did they learn that Plymouth was built on a
site of the extinct Patuxet tribe of which he was the sole survivor

[15] Dexter, op. cit., pp. 3-5.

[16] Bradford, op. cit., Vol. I, p. 164; Rutman, "The Pilgrims and Their Harbor,"
p. 181. It is also probable that the immediate exposure of the harbor to the ocean was
part of the rejection because of fear of foreign attack. See Morton, op. cit., p. 35.

[17] Bradford, op. cit., Vol. I, pp. 231-32; Morton, op. cit., p. 33.

[18] Cushman, Robert, The First Sermon Ever Preached in New England (New York:
J. E. D. Comstock, 1858), p. xiii; Dermer's letter to Samuel Purchas in Burrage, H. S.
(ed.), Gorges and the Grant of the Province of Maine 1622 (Augusta: by the State of Maine,
1923), p. 9; Kittredge, Henry C., Cape Cod (Boston: Houghton Mifflin, 1968), pp. 47-49.
Morton, op. cit., p. 28, attributed the depopulation to an act of God preparing the way for
the Pilgrims.

[19] Gorges, Ferdinando, America Painted to the Life (London: Nath. Brook, 1658-59),
p. 27; Mather, op. cit., Vol. I, p. 51; Morton, op. cit., p. 12; Pory, op. cit., p. 36.

(Figure 16).[20]

The Pilgrims during their initial experiences in New England had mixed feelings about the native population: fearful, curious, yet hopeful of information to aid their settlement.[21] The Pilgrim fear of the natives, for the most part, proved groundless, for on the three discoveries the few remaining Indians avoided the new-comers and attacked them only once on the third discovery. Wheth-er or not the Pilgrims knew why their predecessors considered the natives treacherous, they later were to enjoy amicable relations with the natives, but as strangers in an unknown land they wisely anticipated assaults and prepared for them. At night on land they arranged their camps ". . . partly to defend them selves from any sudden assaults of the savages, if they should surround them. . . ."[22] Another example of their fear occurred after their first difficult night time entrance into Plymouth Bay when ". . . some would keepe the boate for fear they might bee amongst the Indians . . . ," but in the morning ". . . found them sellves to be on an iland secure from the Indeans. . . ."[23] Cushman concluded, "they [Indians] were wont to be most cruel and treacherous people in all these parts . . . but to us they have been like lambs. . . ."[24]

The early attention which the Pilgrims gave to features of native habitation indicated that they were prepared to be guided partially in their site selection by the evidence of Indian land use practices when those were comparable to the Pilgrim. Smith used that principle as the basis of his favorable assessment of Massa-chusetts Bay; the Pilgrims implemented it. On their traverses they noted areas of Indian cultivation. In some instances the fields

---

[20]Dexter, op. cit., pp. 84-85.

[21]Pilgrim curiosity about the American aborigine was limited but exemplified by their wonderment on the emptiness of the habitation sites, on the origin and uses of struc-tures and implements, and on the meaning of the caches and burial practices. Since that curiosity does not directly relate to their locational decisions, it will not be developed here. See Dexter, op. cit., pp. 20, 21, 35, or 49, for examples.

[22]Bradford, op. cit., Vol. I, pp. 170-71; Morison (ed.), op. cit., p. 69.

[23]Bradford, op. cit., Vol. I, pp. 175-76; Morison (ed.), op. cit., p. 71.

[24]Cushman, op. cit., p. xiii. See Langdon, op. cit., for a full discussion of Pilgrim-Indian relations.

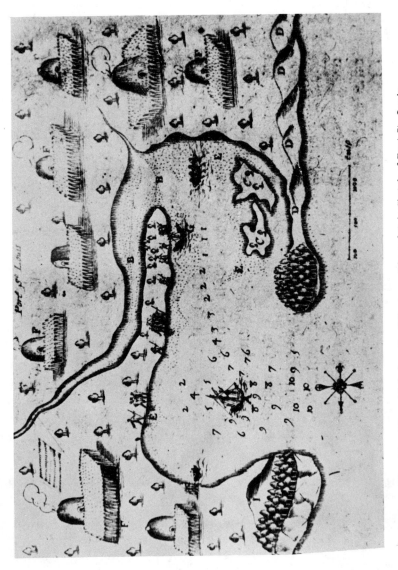

Fig. 16. --Plymouth before the Pilgrims: Champlain's Sketch of Port St. Louis

had been unused in the seasons immediately prior to the Pilgrim arrival, but the association in the Pilgrim mind with agricultural potential was clear. ". . . From thence we went on & found much plaine ground, about fiftie Acres, fit for the Plow, and some signes where the Indians had formerly planted their corne. . . ."[25] Less frequently seen were recently harvested fields. "We went on further and found new stubble, of which they had gotten Corne this yeare, and many Walnut trees full of Nuts, and great store of Strawberries, and some Vines; passing thus a field or two, which were not great, we came to another, which had also bin new gotten, and there we found where an house had beene. . . also we found a great Ketle, which had beene some Ships ketle and brought out of Europe."[26]

Indian clearings were valued not only because they would require less work to convert into fields but also because they were considered to be more defensible than densely timbered areas. One site was judged ". . . so incompassed with woods, that we should bee in much danger of the Salvages, and our number being so little, and so much ground to cleare, so as we thought good to quit and cleare that place, till we were of more strength. . . ."[27] Another was ". . . so full of wood, as we could hardly cleare so much to serue vs for Corne. . . ."[28]

The Pilgrims at first gave no indication that they knew how those clearings were created. Later contacts revealed the Indian burning practices,[29] which Thomas Morton, an Englishman who arrived in Massachusetts in 1622, described.[30]

---

[25] Dexter, op. cit., pp. 19, 49, 61. Quoted passage is on p. 19.

[26] Ibid., pp. 20-21. Reference to strawberries must be to the plants rather than the fruit because of the season, or the Pilgrims inaccurately identified the plant.

[27] Ibid., p. 63. Meaning of the second "cleare" in this passage is to leave or vacate.

[28] Ibid., p. 64.   [29] Ibid., p. 75.

[30] Morton, Thomas, The New English Canaan (Boston: Prince Society, 1883), p. 172. It is of interest to observe that Morton did not associate the practice with either hunting or cultivation as do modern students of Indian life. See Day, Gordon M., "The Indian as an Ecological Factor in the Northeastern Forest," Ecology, XXXIV (April, 1953), 334-39, and Driver, Harold E., Indians of North America (Chicago: University of Chicago Press, 1961), pp. 51-52.

The Salvages are accustomed to set fire to the Country in all places where they come, and to burne it twize a yeare, viz: at the Spring, and the fall of the leafe. The reason that moves them to doe so, is because it would other wise be so overgrowne with underweedes that it would be all a coppice wood, and the people would not be able in any wise to passe through the Country out of a beaten path.

Later Englishmen often viewed the evidence of Indian agriculture and clearing much as the Pilgrims did. Christopher Levett detailed those features among his reasons for selecting a satisfactory settlement site. "There I think a good plantation may be settled, for there is . . . good ground, and much already cleared, fit for planting corne and other fruits, having heretofore ben planted by the Salvages who are all dead."[31]

Another feature of the Indian landscape which the Pilgrims used were trails and paths. ". . . We followed certaine beaten paths and trails of the Indians into the Woods. . . ."[32] When they were not followed, the explorers were apt to be ". . . shrewdly pusled, and lost our way, as we wandred. . . ."[33] But however convenient the Pilgrims might have found the trails, Indian movement patterns did not play any direct or significant role in the site choice.

Pilgrim observation of natural features was utilitarian as one might expect in the critical circumstances of finding a satisfactory site in a short time. As recorded in Mourt's Relation those observations were limited almost exclusively to the phenomena necessitous to their way of life and exiled status. Among the high priority characteristics for the settlement site was a usable harbor deep enough for ocean ships but with inshore depths to allow shore landing or wharves. It also needed to be sheltered from storms but not barred to hinder egress or ingress and be defensible from attack by foreign ships. Either a small bay or a navigable river would satisfy those criteria. Both types were considered by the Pilgrims. ". . . But we found it onely to be a Bay, without either river or creeke comming into it, yet we deemed it to be as good an harbour as Cape Cod, for they that found it, found a ship might

---

[31]Baxter, J. P. (ed.), Christopher Levett of York (Portland: Gorges Society, 1893), p. 93.

[32]Dexter, op. cit., p. 32.   [33]Ibid., p. 24.

ride in fiue fathom water. . . ."[34] Pamet River, however, was
unsuitable because it was unnavigable and too shallow for landing
of ocean ships.[35]

Their concept of arable land linked soil fertility and terrain.
The Pilgrims preferred level areas for their fields as suggested
by their rejection of one site ". . . because many liked not the
hillinesse of the soyle. . . ."[36] Elsewhere two areas were described without negative features, but it was the one with level
ground that was labeled ". . . fit for the plow. . . ."[37] Another
site had ". . . a levill soyle, but none of the fruitfullest. . . ."[38]
The rockiness of New England soils did not escape the newcomers'
eyes. "In some places its very rockie both aboue ground and in
it."[39] Later after trials with cultivation they were able to make
comparative assessments. "The soyle at Nauset and here is alike,
even and sandy, not so good for corne as where we are. . . ." Only
infrequently was an evaluation of soil fertility based on soil color.[40]

The utilitarian assessment of the landscape also prevailed in
the flora which were cataloged in <u>Mourt's Relation</u>. The familiar
and usable dominated, but unrecognized species were occasionally
listed. Oak, pine, walnut, sassafras, juniper, ash, and birch, all
of which had some known practical use, were the trees most frequently listed. The density of the trees was a matter of concern,
for the Pilgrims were fearful of settling in too dense woodlands.
They preferred either clearings with timber nearby or ". . . wood
for the most open and without underwood, fit either to goe or ride
in. . . ."[41] "And though the Countrey bee wilde and over-growne
with woods, yet the trees stand not thicke, but a man may well
ride a horse amongst them."[42]

Lower plants and shrubs included vines, holly, various berries, herbs, and grasses. ". . . All Spring time the earth sendeth

[34] <u>Ibid</u>., p. 47.

[35] <u>Ibid</u>., pp. 29, 38.

[36] <u>Ibid</u>., p. 30.

[37] <u>Ibid</u>., p. 20.

[38] <u>Ibid</u>., p. 47.

[39] <u>Ibid</u>., p. 105.

[40] <u>Ibid</u>., pp. 10, 117.

[41] <u>Ibid</u>., p. 10.

[42] <u>Ibid</u>., p. 105.

forth naturally very good Sallet herbs; here are Grapes, white and red, and very sweete and strong also. Strawberries, Gooseberries, Raspas, & Plums of three sorts, with blacke and red, being almost as good as Damsen: abundance of Roses, white, red, and damask: single, but very sweet. . . ."[43]

Because of arrival when cultivation was impossible for several months and the limited food supplies on the _Mayflower_, understandably the Pilgrims gave immediate attention to the area's hunting potential. However, in the settlement choice greater emphasis was placed on the arable needs rather than hunting, a circumstance which was consistent with the future agricultural nature of Pilgrim society.[44] Also the Cape might have been as devoid of animals as it was of Indians in that late Fall when the Pilgrims first explored, for deer were the only large land animals mentioned with any frequency.[45] The adversity of nature was evidenced by the presence of wolves.[46] Fur bearing animals, whose pelts the Pilgrims later sought as far distant as the Kennebec and the Connecticut Valley, were infrequently mentioned in the text of _Mourt's Relation_, a mystifying status because the Pilgrims initially hoped that furs would be a major export commodity to pay their English creditors. But one is reminded of Smith's warning that furring would be unrewarding on that section of the New England coast. One of the first mentions of beaver was an early visit to Massachusetts Bay to trade for their pelts.[47]

Wild fowl were abundant and included partridges, flocks of geese and ducks, cranes, and eagles. Local fish, from which a

---

[43]_Ibid._, p. 136.

[44]Demos, John, _A Little Commonwealth: Family Life in Plymouth Colony_ (New York: Oxford University Press, 1970), pp. 13-14.

[45]Dexter, _op. cit._, pp. 17-18, 24. On the other hand the Indian depopulation with its accompanying decline of hunting and clearing should have permitted an increase in the animal population.

[46]_Ibid._, p. 77.

[47]Bradford, _op. cit._, Vol. I, p. 229; Dexter, _op. cit._, p. 57; Winslow, E., _Good News from New England_ in Arber, E. (ed.), _The Story of the Pilgrim Fathers_ (London: Ward and Downey, 1897), p. 521. That trip also offered the first suggestion that the Pilgrims might not have chosen the best possible location for their colony. ". . And made reporte of the place, wishing they had been ther seated. . . ." Bradford, _loc. cit._

profit was expected but never realized, were adequate for food and fertilizing needs, however unsatisfactory the supply might have been for commerce. Besides fish from the bays catch was also available from the inland ponds and streams. Lobsters, eels, and oysters were part of the catch.[48]

Fresh water was a necessity of natural occurrence on which the Pilgrims were completely dependent. Areas where fresh surface water was unobservable were as unattractive as those with it were possible sites.[49] Springs, ponds, and streams were the sources of saltless water considered by the Pilgrim with a combination of any two being preferred because it implied a more abundant and steadier supply than any of the possible sources singularly. In general all were numerous on the Cape and around Plymouth. ". . . Yet the Country so well watered that a man could scarce be drie, but he should haue a spring at hand to coole his thirst, beside smal Rivers in abundance. . . ."[50]

The values which the Pilgrims individually and collectively put on those cultural and natural factors to reach a summary assessment or evaluation of the sites which had been seen is probably best abstracted from the characteristics of the site ultimately selected. However, summation of the debate which ensued at the end of the second discovery revealed both the differences of opinion among the group and the priorities which guided their decisions.[51]

Having thus discovered this place, it was controversall amongst us, what to doe touching our . . . setling there; some thought it best for many reasons to abide there. As first, that there was a convenient Harbour for Boates, though not for ships. Secondly, Good Corne ground readie to our hands, as we saw by experience in the goodly corne it yeelded . . . Thirdly, Cape Cod was like to be a place of good fishing, for we saw daily great Whales of the best kind for oyle and bone, come close aboord our Ship . . . Fourthly, the place was likely to be healthfull, secure, and defensible. But the last and especiall reason was, that now the heart of Winter and unseasonable weather was come upon us. . . .

Others againe urged greatly the going to <u>Anguum</u> or <u>Angoum</u>, a place twentie leagues off to the Northwards, which they had heard to be an excellent harbour for ships; better ground and better fishing. Secondly, for any thing we knew, there might be hard

---

[48]Dexter, <u>op. cit.</u>, pp. 24, 60, 64-65, 70, 82, 101, 125; Pory, <u>op. cit.</u>, pp. 37-40.

[49]Dexter, <u>op. cit.</u>, p. 17.

[50]<u>Ibid.</u>, p. 104. The value here placed on a spring of water anticipated Winthrop's later preference for Shawmut Peninsula (Boston) because of a spring there.

[51]<u>Ibid.</u>, pp. 38-41.

by us a farre better seate, and it should be a great hindrance to seate where we should remoue againe. Thirdly, the water was but in pondes, and it was thought there would be none in Summer, or very little. Fourthly the water there must be fetched up a steepe hill: but to omit many reasons used heere abouts; It was in the ende concluded, to make some discovery within the Bay. . . .

The second phase ended with the selection of Plymouth Bay as the general locale of the colony. Provincetown, Pamet, and Well-fleet were rejected. The advantages of Plymouth in contrast to Provincetown were the former's more suitable harbor because of closer landings and the presence of all immediately necessary items such as water and timber. Pamet was unacceptable because of its small shallow harbor while Wellfleet was burdened by limited fresh water and soil of doubted fertility.[52] In that comparative context Plymouth Bay on most counts was the superior locale. Its advantages were the large sheltered and defensible harbor and on the surrounding shores plenty of water in ponds or streams, trees and plants of practical uses, abundant game, fish, and fowl, both timbered and cleared areas, and evidence of earlier Indian culti-vation.[53]

. . . We sounded the Harbour, and found it a very good Harbour for our shipping, we marched also into the Land, and found divers corne fields, and little running brooks, a place very good for scituation . . . This Harbour is a Bay greater then Cape Cod, compassed with a goodly Land . . . a most hopefull place, innumerable store of fowle, and . . . cannot but bee of fish in their season . . . We marched along the coast in the woods, some 7 or 8 mile, but saw not an Indian nor an Indian house, only we found where formerly, had been some Inhabitants, and where they had planted their corne: we found not any Navigable River, but 4 or 5 small running brookes of very sweet fresh water, that all run into the Sea: The land for the crust of the earth is a spits depth, excellent blacke mold and fat in some places, 2 or 3 great Oakes but not very thicke, Pines, Wal-nuts Beech Ash, Birch, Hasell, Holley, Asp, Sasifras, in abun-dance, & Vines euery where, Cherry trees, Plum-trees, and many other which we know not; many kinds of hearbes, we found heere in Winter. . . .

Such was the initial Pilgrim version of the land which they had chosen for their new homeland.

After the general locale of the colony had been determined the Pilgrims gave their attention to the selection of the specific site of their settlement. Three areas were considered: Plymouth, Jones River, and Clark's Island.[54] Jones River was assessed and

---

[52]Rutman, "The Pilgrims and Their Harbor," p. 181.

[53]Dexter, op. cit., pp. 59-65. Quoted passage is on pp. 59-62.

[54]There is nothing in Mourt's Relation to suggest that other sites around Plymouth Bay were considered.

rejected. The water level was too shallow at low tide, and ". . .
it was so farre from our fishing our principall profit, and so incompassed with woods, that we should bee in much danger of the Salvages . . . and so much ground to cleare, so as we thought good to
quit . . . that place, till we were of more strength. . . ." Clark's
Island, where the exploring party stayed that first night in the bay,
was a possibility because they thought its insularity offered more
security than a mainland site. Investigation revealed no other
attractions. It lacked surface water, had much rocky soil besides
being ". . . judged it colde for our Corne," and was heavily wooded
without clearings or evidence of Indian agriculture. [55]

The final choice was between Plymouth and Jones River. Unable to continue the search because of supply shortages, the Pilgrims chose Plymouth. [56]

> . . . So well as we could we came to a conclusion, by most voyces, to set on the main
> Land, on the first place, on an high ground, where there is a great deale of Land
> cleared, and hath been planted with Corne three or four yeares agoe, and there is a
> very sweet brooke runnes vnder the hill side, and many delicate springs of as good
> water as can be drunke, and where we may harbour our Shallops and Boates exceeding
> well, and in this brooke much good fish in their seasons: on the further side of the
> river also much Corne ground cleared, in one field is a great hill, on which wee poynt
> to make a platforme, and plant our Ordinance, which will command all round about,
> from thence we may see into the Bay, and farre into the Sea, and we may see thence
> Cape Cod: our greatest labour will be fetching of our wood, which is halfe a quarter
> of an English myle, but there is enough so farre off; what people inhabite here we yet
> know not, for as yet we haue seene none, so there we made our Randevous, and a
> place for some of our people about twentie, resolving in the morning to come all
> ashore and to build houses. . . .

The first successful English settlement in New England was under-
way.

The selection of where they would live was made. The English
exiles began to build their village, and its houses would be the
homes of the first English families to live in New England. Tragic-
ally half of their original numbers died during the ensuing winter.
But by the survival of their experiment they proved to a doubtful
audience that the area was habitable by Europeans. They came to
doubt the wisdom of their original site choice made under the pres-

---

[55] Ibid., pp. 63-64.

[56] Ibid., pp. 64-65. Experience proved the Pilgrims wrong on the suitability of
Plymouth harbor because only small boats could dock directly at shore. Ships of the draft
of the Mayflower had to anchor some distance from the shore, a situation which hampered
later Plymouth commerce.

sure of their late arrival, but the site was not abandoned like
Jamestown.[57] Within a decade Plymouth was overshadowed by its
more powerful, populous, and affluent Puritan neighbors. But the
achievement of Plymouth remained. The Pilgrims had demonstrated
to all latercomers that a _new_ England was possible in North Vir-
vinia, the coast renamed by John Smith New England.

---

[57]Morton, N., _op. cit._, p. 121.

CONCLUSION

In the aftermath of the Columbian discovery of the New World Western Europeans were presented with a unique and unprecedented situation, the task of perceiving and assessing a world area of undetermined size whose existence and characteristics had been totally unknown to them and the latter learned only through centuries of arduous exploration. The entire experience provides a vast laboratory in which to study many aspects of cultural geography, but here only one is defined as the focus of investigation--the changing impressions made by alien groups of a newly discovered part of the world. For this monograph one New World section, the New England coast of the United States, from the dawning of European knowledge of its existence until the time when its permanent settlement was begun by them has been selected to examine selected aspects of the interlocking relationships among image, area, and group behavior. Because it stresses data of a specific part of the earth's surface, it is a study in regional geographic history; because it is concerned with areal impressions and imagery, it has broad import to cultural geography as an investigation of human group perception and assessment of the earth's environments.

The central concern is what Europeans at a certain period thought the region was like, not what it in fact might have been. The appraisals of the area which were contained in various images had two basic phases of formation. The area's landscape content first had to be obtained and perceived and, secondly, assessed in terms of the perceiving group. A critical restriction inherent to the historical nature of the study is the character and amount of surviving materials. During the period of this study only a small minority of Europeans directly experienced the New World, and of those the portion who visited the New England coast was very small. Of those visitors only a limited number recorded in some fashion what they saw, what they made of the landscape which they viewed, and why it was interpreted as it was. That small supply of direct perception of the region was the source from which fact and misconception about the area were diffused to a larger audience.

A fortuitous exception to the evidence lacuna is New World cartography. Enough maps survive to document the progression of the study area over the period of its emergence from unknown status to its portrayal with a realistic coastal configuration. Maps not only provide a graphic record of the images which developed but also illustrate the successive stages and changes of knowledge and conceptions which evolved during the study period. From those maps a variety of information about Europeans' thoughts and conceptions of New England may be obtained. The teleological framework of the cartographer was sometimes as apparent as was the sum of his specific knowledge of the area. Preconceptions were particularly important when data were meager or lacking as attempts to define the area's relationship to the remainder of the world illustrated. Depending on the cartographer's conceptions or data, the coast was shown either as continental or insular. While less preconception is observable in arrangements of the coast's bays and peninsulas, interior stream patterns were omitted by some cartographers, but others less carefully drew them with sources close to a western ocean or in large lakes, or as riverine straits. Some cartographers were very critical in analysis of data and attempted to identify comparable phenomena recorded in different sources, but others created and augmented confusion by unquestioned duplication of regional features. Technical limitations as well as the character of reports were seen in persistent errors of latitude and longitude, although the tendency of indifferent cartographers to copy predecessors' drawings quickly led to perpetuation of stereotypes such as a lengthy east-west coastline after evidence was available to correct misconceptions. Other than conceptual biases, political ones were important. Nationalistic cartographic traditions tended to sustain national policy and its associated claims, and since nationals like the Italians who were not competitors in the New World drew their data from the conflicting nations, the nationalistic overtones were both direct and indirect. The ultimate emergence of realistic map images early in the seventeenth century illustrated how crucially their accuracy depended on the drawer's astuteness as a collector or compiler of data, his skill as a cartographer, and his purpose for making the map.

Cartographic materials were both a source and an outcome of a late Elizabethan venture to formulate the first composite image of the area before a settlement scheme was formulated. But in the purposive effort to obtain as much data for the area as were available, documentation was not limited to maps. With the benefits of hindsight the modern researcher is aware of the meager and often fancifully inaccurate information which the planners of the Norembega scheme had; however, beyond the materials which they collected and examined, they had no resources to separate fact from fancy because of the sparsity of available data. Their efforts were an early example of an attempt to validate the accuracy of an areal image. The examiners were men of high officialdom, wealthy merchant investors, and a representative of the dynamic Elizabethan courtier, if in this case an incompetent leader. However vague and inadequate was its factual base, the image was considered to be favorable, and their sponsorship of the scheme illustrated the role of an areal image in subsequent action. The colonial scheme was both a product of its creators' designs and the nature of their England. It was anachronistic in that it envisioned the establishment of feudal settlement and land tenure practices then undergoing change and futuristic in that as an early manifestation of mercantilistic economic philosophy the colony was hoped to produce commodities needed in England as well as strategic advantages for England.

A later French image retained several important themes as found in the Elizabethan Norembega image, but the idea of a permanent, overseas self-sustaining colony was conspicuously absent. The French image was more obviously mercantilistic and had a more rigidly defined economic focus. The area was evaluated against the background of a then novel conception of one type of commerce--a long term, sustained fur trade with a permanent collection and export station accessible to a collection region exclusively under French control. Like the Elizabethan backers of Gilbert's scheme developers of the French plan were a national sub-group, and the region's potentialities for anything other than the immediate interests of that sub-group did not enter into its final assessment, although their decisions and image would later play an important role in French national policy toward the area. In contrast to the Elizabethan image which was constructed from afar, the French for their decisions not only had the results of longer and direct experience but also more accurate and abundant knowledge. The data collection and assessment phases were conducted almost simultaneously. Systematic exploration of the coast, highly perceptive observation of its cultural and physical geography, and a precisely defined purpose gave validity and consistency to the French image and its developmental processes unique to the time, but prophetic of procedures and relationships which marked the better expansion schemes in later centuries.

Concurrent with the French activities but more decisive because they were the immediate antecedents of the New England which has developed into modern times was the reappearance of Englishmen on New England's coast. Their motives included the advancement of national prestige and fish and fur collection from the coast and its waters. Exploration of the coast was less systematic than the French had undertaken, and data and assessments were enveloped in promotional language and literature. The frustration of an abortive plan to place a post on the coast was mitigated by the lure of profit from exploitation of the area's resources. Establishment and rapid abandonment of another post introduced an image dominated by the idea that the area was uninhabitable by Englishmen. Explanation of that colonial failure is complex; partial knowledge of the area's climate, inadequate preparations, and ineffectual leadership all contributed. But with human predilection to assign a singular cause to events, the harsh winter conditions of the area were made the reason for colonial failure and rationale why future permanent European residence was precluded. It is an example of how in image formation one event may unpredictably alter established lines of development and substitute unforeseen ones. The evidence of economic profit, however, encouraged some people to retain the older exploitive image and its contacts.

Promoters were a consistent factor in the creation of English impressions of the region. Their role was generally positive and encouraged more active relationships between the New England region and their homeland, but even they were unable to alter the prevalence of the non-settlement image until time ameliorated the initial adverse reactions. Promotion like all human endeavors attracts a range of talents. The immediate pre-settlement image of New England was fortunate that it was the instrument of one of history's most talented promoters, Captain John Smith. His argument that the area could be inhabited by Englishmen went beyond his predecessors' claims of a bountiful and attractive land to stress the example of the large indigenous population which the area sustained but which failed to realize the potential of the area as Englishmen would. But even he failed to attract sponsors or settlers to carry out his dreams.

Example, not words, was needed to convince Englishmen that their relationship to the region could include a resident overseas population involved in activities other than exploitive export trade. Events of the era provided that example independently of promotional efforts. A group of Englishmen who found themselves on its southern coast chose the area as the locale for their settlement. Primary considerations became the human will to endure and ability of humans to exist under adverse and uncontrollable conditions and circumstances. The necessity of their immediate survival dictated that the Pilgrims settle where they had not intended in a region branded as inhospitable and uninhabitable. Like the French before them, the phases of perception and assessment were done simultaneously but for different reasons. Limited exploration of the small portion of the coast accessible to them was followed by group decisions which established their settlement site. The continuance of their settlement demonstrated the validity of promoters' image that Englishmen would flourish on that coast despite its drawbacks.

BIBLIOGRAPHY

Primary Sources

Arber, E. (ed.). The First Three English Books on America. Birmingham: n.p., 1885.

_____. The Story of the Pilgrim Fathers. London: Ward and Downey, 1897.

_____. Travels and Works of Captain John Smith. 2 vols. Edinburgh: John Grant, 1910.

Banks, Charles E. "New Documents Relating to the Popham Expedition." Proceedings of the American Antiquarian Society, New Series, XXXIX (October, 1929), 307-34.

Barlow, Roger. A Brief Summe of Geographie. London: Hakluyt Society, 1932.

Bacchiani, Alessandro. "Giovanni da Verazzano and His Discoveries in North America 1524." Annual Report of the American Scenic and Historic Preservation Society, XV (1910), 135-226.

Baxter, James P. (ed.). Christopher Levett of York. Portland: Gorges Society, 1893.

_____. Sir Ferdinando Gorges and His Province of Maine. 3 vols. Boston: Prince Society, 1890.

Biggar, H. P. (ed.). The Precursors of Jacques Cartier 1497-1534. Vol. V. of Publications of the Canadian Archives. Ottawa: Government Printing House, 1911.

_____. A Collection of Documents Relating to Jacques Cartier and the Sieur de Roberval. Vol. XIV of Publications of the Public Archives of Canada. Ottawa: Public Archives of Canada, 1930.

_____. The Works of Samuel de Champlain. 6 vols. Toronto: Champlain Society, 1922-36.

Bradford, William. History of Plymouth Plantation 1620-1647. 2 vols. Boston: Massachusetts Historical Society, 1912.

Brown, Alexander. The Genesis of the United States. 2 vols. New York: Russell & Russell, 1964. Reprint of 1890 edition.

Burrage, Henry S. (ed.). Gorges and the Grant of the Province of Maine 1622. Augusta: printed for the state of Maine, 1923.

Calendar of State Papers: Colonial Series. London: H. M. Stationery Office, 1860. Vol. I.

Champlain, Samuel de. Champlain's Voyages. 3 vols. Boston: Prince Society, 1878-82.

Cogswell, Joseph G. "The Voyage of John de Verazzano along the Coast of North America from Carolina to Newfoundland A.D. 1524." Collections of the New York Historical Society, 2nd Series, I (1841), 37-67.

Colombo-Vespucci-Verazzano. Turin: L'Unione Tipografico-Editrice Torinese, 1966.

Cortesão, Armando, and da Mota, Avelino T. Portugaliae Monumenta Cartographica. 5 vols. Lisbon: n.p., 1960.

Cushman, Robert. The First Sermon Ever Preached in New England. New York: J. E. D. Comstock, 1858.

Deane, Charles. "Documents Relating to the Expeditions of Captain Samuel Argall." Proceedings of the Massachusetts Historical Society, 2nd Series, I (1884-85), 187-92.

Dexter, H. M. (ed.). Mourt's Relation or a Journal of the Plantation at Plymouth. Boston: John K. Wiggin, 1865.

Fite, E. D., and Freeman, A. A Book of Old Maps Delineating American History from the Earliest Days down to the Close of the Revolutionary War. Cambridge: Harvard University Press, 1926.

Fuller, Thomas. The History of the Worthies of England. 3 vols. London: J. G. W. L. and W. G., 1662.

Galvano, Antonio. The Discoveries of the World. London: Hakluyt Society, 1857. Reprint of 1563 edition.

Gomara, Francisco Lopez de. Historia General de las Indias. 2 vols. Madrid: Calpe, 1922. Reprint of 1552 edition.

Gorges, Ferdinando. America Painted to the Life. London: Nath. Brook, 1658-59.

Hakluyt, Richard. Divers Voyages Touching the Discoverie of America. London: G. Woodcocke, 1582. Reprinted Ann Arbor: University Microfilms, 1966.

_____. The Principall Navigations Voiages and Discoveries of the English Nation. 2 vols. Cambridge: Cambridge University Press, 1965. Facsimile reprint of 1589 edition.

_____. The Principal Navigations Voyages Traffiques & Discoveries of the English Nation. 12 vols. Glasgow: James Maclehose and Sons, 1903-5. Reprint of 1598-1600 edition.

Halliwell, James C. (ed.). The Private Diary of Dr. John Dee. London: Camden Society, 1842.

Hamor, Ralph. A True Discourse of the Present State of Virginia. London: John Beals, 1615.

Heath, Dwight B. (ed.). A Journal of the Pilgrims at Plymouth. New York: Corinth Books, 1963.

Josselyn, John. An Account of Two Voyages to New-England. London: G. Widdowes, 1675. Reprinted in Collections of the Massachusetts Historical Society, 3rd Series, III (1833), 211-396.

_____. New-Englands Rarities. London: G. Widdowes, 1672. Reprinted in Archaeologia Americana, IV (1860), 133-238.

Kohl, J. G. Descriptive Catalogue of Those Maps, Charts and Surveys Relating to America. Washington: Henry Polkinhorn, 1857.

Kunstmann, Friedrich. Die Entdeckung Amerikas und Atlas. München and Berlin: In Commission bei A. Asher & Cie, 1859.

Lafréry, Antoine. Geografica tavole moderne di Geografia. Rome, 1575.

Levermore, Charles H. (ed.). Forerunners and Competitors of the Pilgrims and Puritans. 2 vols. Brooklyn: New England Society of Brooklyn, 1912.

MacNutt, F. A. (ed.). De Orbe Novo: The Eight Decades of Peter Martyr d'Anghiera. 2 vols. New York: G. P. Putnam's Sons, 1912.

Magnusson, M., and Palsson, H. (ed.). The Vinland Sagas: The Norse Discovery of America. Baltimore: Penguin Books, 1965.

Maverick, Samuel. "A Briefe Discription of New England and the Severall Townes Therein. " Proceedings of the Massachusetts Historical Society, 2nd Series, I (October, 1884), 231-49.

Monardes, Nicholas, and Frampton, John. Joyfull Newes out of the New Founde Worlde. New York: Alfred A. Knopf, 1925. Reprint of 1577 London edition.

Morison, Samuel E. (ed.). Of Plymouth Plantation 1620-1647. New York: Random House-Modern Library, 1952.

Morton, Nathaniel. New-Englands Memoriall. Boston: Club of Odd Volumes, 1903. Reprint of 1669 edition.

Morton, Thomas. The New English Canaan. Boston: Prince Society, 1883.

Nordenskiöld, N. A. E. Facsimile Atlas. Stockholm: P. A. Norstedt & söner, 1889.

_____. Perpiplus: An Essay on the Early History of Charts and Sailing Directions. Stockholm: P. A. Norstedt & söner, 1897.

O'Callaghan, E. B. (ed.). Documents Relative to the Colonial History of the State of New York. 10 vols. Albany: Weed, Parsons and Company, 1858.

Percy, George. "A Trewe Relacyon. " Tyler's Quarterly, III (1922), 259-82.

Pory, John. John Pory's Lost Description of Plymouth Colony. Boston: Houghton, Mifflin, 1918.

Ptolemy, Claudius. Geografia. Rome, 1508.

_____. Geografia. Venice, 1548.

_____. Geografia. Venice, 1561.

Purchas, Samuel. Hakluytus Posthumus or Purchas His Pilgrimes. 20 vols. New York: AMS Press, 1965.

Quinn, David B. (ed.). The Roanoke Voyages 1584-1590. 2 vols. London: Hakluyt Society, 1955.

_____. The Voyages and Colonising Enterprises of Sir Humphrey Gilbert. 2 vols. London: Hakluyt Society, 1940.

Ramusio, Giovanni. Terzo Volvme delle Navigationi et Viaggi. Venice: Stamperia de Givnti, 1556.

"Records of the New England Company." Proceedings of the American Antiquarian Society, XLVII (April, 1867), 53-131.

Remarkable Maps of the XVth, XVIth, and XVIIth Centuries. 4 vols. Amsterdam: Frederik Muller, 1894-97.

Sir William Alexander and American Colonization. Boston: Prince Society, 1873.

Skelton, R. A. Decorative Printed Maps of the 15th to 18th Centuries. London: Spring Books, 1952.

Skelton, R. A., et al. Vinland Map and Tartar Relation. New Haven: Yale University Press, 1964.

Slafter, Carlos (ed.). Sir Humfrey Gylberte and His Enterprise of Colonization in America. Boston: Prince Society, 1903.

Strachey, William. The History of Travell into Virginia Britania. London: Hakluyt Society, 1952.

Taylor, E. G. R. (ed.). The Original Writings and Correspondence of the Two Richard Hakluyts. 2 vols. London: Hakluyt Society, 1935.

Thayer, Henry O. (ed.). The Sagadahoc Colony. Portland: Gorges Society, 1892.

Thevet, André. The New Founde Worlde or Antarctike. London: T. Hacket for Henrie Bynneman, 1568.

Thwaites, R. G. (ed.). The Jesuit Relations and Allied Documents. New York: Pageant Book Company, 1959. Vols. I-IV.

"Tracts Appended to Brereton." Collections of the Massachusetts Historical Society, 3rd Series, VIII (1843), 94-123.

Vigneras, L. A. "New Light on the 1497 Cabot Voyage to America." Hispanic American Historical Review, XXXVI (1956), 503-9.

Williamson, J. A. (ed.). The Cabot Voyages and Bristol Discovery under Henry VII. Cambridge: University Press for the Hakluyt Society, 1962.

Winsor, Justin (ed.). The Kohl Collection of Maps Relating to America. Washington: Government Printing Office, 1904.

Winthrop Papers. 5 vols. Boston: Massachusetts Historical Society, 1929-47.

Wytfliet, Cornelius à. Descriptionis Ptolemaicae Augmentum. Louvain: J. Boogaard, 1597.

Young, Alexander (ed.). Chronicles of the First Planters of the Colony of Massachusetts Bay. Boston: Charles C. Little and James Brown, 1846.

_____ (ed.). Chronicles of the Pilgrim Fathers. Boston: Charles C. Little and James Brown, 1841.

Secondary Sources

Andrews, Charles M. The Colonial Period of American History. 4 vols. New Haven: Yale University Press, 1934-38.

Bagrow, Leo. History of Cartography. London: C. A. Watts & Co., 1964.

Barbour, Philip L. The Three Worlds of Captain John Smith. London: Macmillan, 1964.

Biddle, Richard. Memoir of Sebastian Cabot. Philadelphia: Carey and Lea, 1831.

Biggar, H. P. The Early Trading Companies of New France. Toronto: University of Toronto Library, 1901.

Bishop, Morris. Champlain: The Life of Fortitude. New York: Alfred A. Knopf, 1948.

Bolton, Charles K. The Real Founders of New England. Boston: F. W. Faxon, 1929.

Buffinton, Arthur H. "New England and the Western Fur Trade, 1629-1675." Publications of the Colonial Society of Massachusetts, XVIII (1915-1916), 160-92.

Burrage, Henry S. The Beginnings of Colonial Maine 1602-1658. Augusta: printed for the state of Maine, 1914.

Carroll, Peter N. Puritanism and the Wilderness. New York: Columbia University Press, 1969.

Clark, Andrew H. Acadia: The Geography of Early Nova Scotia to 1760. Madison: University of Wisconsin Press, 1968.

Clarke, J. S. The Progress of Maritime Discovery. London: T. Cadell & W. Davies, 1803.

Coleman, R. V. The First Frontier. New York: Charles Scribner's Sons, 1948.

Cortesão, Armando. "Note on the Castiglioni Planisphere." Imago Mundi, XI (1954), 53-55.

Crone, G. R. Maps and Their Makers. London: Hutchinson & Co., 1968.

Dahlgren, E. W. Map of Santa Cruz. Stockholm: Swedish Staff-General, 1892.

Davies, Arthur. "The 'English' Coast on the Map of Juan de la Cosa." Imago Mundi, XII (1956), 26-29.

Day, Gordon M. "The Indian as an Ecological Factor in the Northeastern Forest." Ecology, XXIV (April, 1953), 334-39.

De Costa, B. F. Ancient Norombega or the Voyages of Simon Ferdinando and John Walker to the Penobscot River 1579-1580. Albany: Joel Munsell's Sons, 1890.

Demos, John. A Little Commonwealth: Family Life in the Plymouth Colony. New York: Oxford University Press, 1970.

Driver, H. E. Indians of North America. Chicago: University of Chicago Press, 1961.

Forster, J. R. History of the Voyages and Discoveries Made in the North. London: G. G. J. and J. Robinson, 1786.

Fussell, G. E. "Social and Agrarian Background of the Pilgrim Fathers." Agricultural History, VIII (1933), 183-202.

Ganong, W. F. Crucial Maps in the Early Cartography and Place-Nomenclature of the Atlantic Coast of Canada. Toronto: University of Toronto Press, 1964.

_____. "The Origin of the Place-Names Acadia and Norumbega." Transactions of the Royal Society of Canada, 3rd Series, XI (1917), Section II, 105-11.

Gilman, Stanwood, and Gilman, Margaret. Land of the Kennebec. Boston: Branden Press, 1966.

Goodwin, W. B. "The Dee River of 1583 and Its Relation to Norumbega." Collections of the Rhode Island Historical Society, XXVII (January, 1934), 38-50.

Gookin, W. F. Bartholomew Gosnold. Hamden, Conn.: Archon Books, 1963.

Gosling, W. G. The Life of Sir Humphrey Gilbert. London: Constable & Co., 1911.

Habert, Jacques. When New York Was Called Angoulême. New York: Transocean Press, 1949.

Harrisse, Henry. The Discovery of North America. Amsterdam: N. Israel, 1961. Reprint of 1892 edition.

Heawood, Edward. "Lopo Homem's Map of 1519." Geographical Journal, LXXVII (March, 1931), 250-55.

Hoffman, Bernard G. Cabot to Cartier: Sources for a Historical Ethnography of North-eastern North America 1497-1550. Toronto: University of Toronto Press, 1961.

Howe, Henry F. Prologue to New England. New York: Farrar & Rinehart, 1943.

Innes, H. A. The Cod Fisheries. New Haven: Yale University Press, 1940.

_____. The Fur Trade in Canada. New Haven: Yale University Press, 1930.

Kittredge, Henry C. Cape Cod. Boston: Houghton, Mifflin, 1968.

Koeman, C. The History of Abraham Ortelius and His Theatrum Orbis Terrum. Lausanne: Sequoia S.A., 1964.

Kohl, J. G. History of the Discovery of Maine. Vol. I of "Documentary History of the State of Maine." Collections of the Maine Historical Society, 2nd Series (1869).

Kroeber, A. L. Cultural and Natural Areas of Native North America. Berkeley: University of California Press, 1939.

Langdon, G. F. Plymouth Colony: A History of New Plymouth 1620-1691. New Haven: Yale University Press, 1966.

Lorant, Stefan. The New World. New York: Duell, Sloan, & Pearce, 1946.

Lounsbury, Ralph G. The British Fishery at Newfoundland 1634-1763. New Haven: Yale University Press, 1934.

Mc Cann, F. T. English Discovery of America to 1585. New York: King's Crown Press of Columbia University, 1952.

Mc Manis, Douglas R. "English Evaluation of North American Iron during the Late Sixteenth and Early Seventeenth Centuries." Professional Geographer, XXI (March, 1969), 93-96.

_____. "The Traditions of Vinland." Annals of the Association of American Geographers, LIX (December, 1969), 797-814.

MacInnes, C. M. A Gateway of Empire. Bristol: J. W. Arrowsmith, 1939.

Mather, Cotton. Magnalia Christi Americana: Or, the Ecclesiastical History of New England. 2 vols. Hartford: Silas Andrus and Son, 1855. Reprint of 1702 London edition.

Morison, Samuel E. The European Discovery of America: The Northern Voyages. New York: Oxford University Press, 1971.

_____. Portuguese Voyages to America in the Fifteenth Century. Cambridge: Harvard University Press, 1940.

Mood, Fulmer. "Narragansett Bay and Dee River, 1583." Collections of the Rhode Island Historical Society, XXVIII (October, 1935), 97-100.

Murphy, Henry C. The Voyage of Verrazzano. New York: n.p., 1875.

Nickerson, W. S. Land Ho!--1620: A Seaman's Story of the Mayflower. Boston: Houghton, Mifflin, 1931.

Notestein, Wallace. The English People on the Eve of Colonization 1603-1630. New York: Harper & Brothers, 1954.

Nunn, G. E. The la Cosa Map and the Cabot Voyages. Jenkintown: Tall Tree Library, 1946.

_____. The Mappemonde of Juan de la Cosa. Jenkintown: George H. Beans Library, 1934.

Oleson, T. J. Early Voyages and Northern Approaches 1000-1632. Toronto: McClellan and Stewart, 1963.

Palfrey, J. G. History of New England. 3 vols. Boston: Little, Brown, 1858.

Parkman, Francis. Pioneers of France in the New World. Boston: Little Brown, 1931.

Parks, George B. Richard Hakluyt and the English Voyages. New York: American Geographical Society, 1928.

Parry, J. H. The Age of Reconnaissance. London: Weidenfeld and Nicolson, 1963.

Patterson, George. "The Portuguese on the North-East Coast of America, and the First European Attempt at Colonization There: A Lost Chapter in American History." Transactions of the Royal Society of Canada (1890), Section II, 127-73.

Pinkerton, John. A General Collection of the Best and Most Interesting Voyages and Travels in All Parts of the World. 17 vols. London: Longman, Hurst, Rees, Orme, and Brown, 1808-14.

Pomfret, John E. Founding the American Colonies 1583-1660. New York: Harper and Row, 1970.

Preston, R. A. Gorges of Plymouth Fort. Toronto: University of Toronto Press, 1953.

Prince, Thomas. A Chronological History of New England. 5 vols. in 1. Edinburgh: privately printed, 1887. Reprint of 1736 Boston edition.

Pring, James H. Captain Martin Pringe: The Last of the Elizabethan Seaman. Plymouth, U.K.: W. H. Luke, 1888.

Quinn, David B. "The Argument for the English Discovery of America between 1480 and 1494." Geographical Journal, CXXVII (1961), 277-85.

_____. "The Voyage of Etienne Bellenger to the Maritimes in 1583: A New Document." Canadian Historical Review, XLIII (1962), 328-43.

Read, Conyers. Mr Secretary Walsingham and the Policy of Queen Elizabeth. 3 vols. New York: Archon Books, 1967. Reprint of 1925 edition.

Reed, Arthur W. "John Rastell's Voyage in the Year 1517." Mariner's Mirror, IX (May, 1923), 137-47.

Roukema, E. "Some Remarks on the La Cosa Map." Imago Mundi, XIV (1959), 38-54.

Rowse, A. L. The Elizabethans and America. London: Macmillan, 1959.

Rozwenc, Edwin C. "Captain John Smith's Image of America." William and Mary Quarterly, 3rd Series, XVI (January, 1959), 27-36.

Rutman, Darrett B. Husbandmen of Plymouth. Boston: Beacon Press, 1967.

_____. "The Pilgrims and Their Harbor." William and Mary Quarterly, 3rd Series, XVII (April, 1960), 164-75.

Sauer, Carl O. "The Settlement of the Humid East." Climate and Man: Yearbook of Agriculture 1940. Washington: Government Printing Office, 1941. Pp. 157-66.

_____. Sixteenth Century North America. Berkeley: University of California Press, 1971.

Shepard, Paul. Man in the Landscape. New York: Alfred A. Knopf, 1964.

Shurtleff, H. R. The Log Cabin Myth. Cambridge: Harvard University Press, 1939.

Skelton, R. A. Explorers' Maps. New York: Frederick A. Praeger, 1958.

Stevenson, E. L. "Early Spanish Cartography of the New World." Proceedings of the American Antiquarian Society, New Series, XIX (1908-9), 369-412.

Stokes, I. N. Phelps. Iconography of Manhattan Island. 6 vols. New York: Robert H. Dodd, 1915-28.

Stith, William. The History of the First Discovery and Settlement of Virginia. Williamsburg: William Parks, 1747.

Taylor, E. G. R. "Instructions to a Colonial Surveyor in 1582." Mariner's Mirror, XXXVII (1951), 48-62.

_____. Late Tudor and Early Stuart Geography 1583-1650. New York: Octagon Books, 1968. Reprint of 1934 edition.

_____. Tudor Geography 1485-1583. New York: Octagon Books, 1968. Reprint of 1930 edition.

Tenison, E. M. Elizabethan England. 12 vols. Royal Leamington Spa: by author, 1933-60.

Tercentenary of Martin Pring's First Voyage to the Coast of Maine 1603-1903. Portland: Maine Historical Society, 1905.

Vigneras, L. A. "The Cartographer Diogo Ribeiro." Imago Mundi, XVI (1962), 76-83.

_____. "The Voyage of Esteban Gomez from Florida to the Baccalaos." Terrae Incognitae, II (1970), 25-28.

Weeden, W. B. Economic and Social History of New England 1620-1789. 2 vols. Boston: Houghton, Mifflin, 1890.

Willison, George F. Behold Virginia! the Fifth Crown. New York: Harcourt, Brace, 1952.

_____. Saints and Strangers. New York: Reynal and Hitchcock, 1945.

Winsor, Justin (ed.). Narrative and Critical History of America. 8 vols. Boston: Houghton, Mifflin, 1884-89.

Wroth, L. C. The Voyages of Giovanni da Verrazzano 1524-1528. New Haven: Yale University Press, 1970.

Yates, F. A. John Florio: The Life of an Italian in Shakespeare's England. Cambridge: Cambridge University Press, 1934.

THE UNIVERSITY OF CHICAGO
DEPARTMENT OF GEOGRAPHY
RESEARCH PAPERS (Lithographed, 6×9 Inches)

(Available from Department of Geography, The University of Chicago, 5828 S. University Ave., Chicago, Illinois 60637. Price: $5.00 each; by series subscription, $4.00 each.)

117. WONG, SHUE TUCK. *Perception of Choice and Factors Affecting Industrial Water Supply Decisions in Northeastern Illinois* 1968. 96 pp.

119. DIENES, LESLIE. *Locational Factors and Locational Developments in the Soviet Chemical Industry* 1969. 285 pp.

120. MIHELIC, DUSAN. *The Political Element in the Port Geography of Trieste* 1969. 104 pp.

121. BAUMANN, DUANE. D. *The Recreational Use of Domestic Water Supply Reservoir: Perception and Choice* 1969. 125 pp.

122. LIND, AULIS O. *Coastal Landforms of Cat Island, Bahamas: A Study of Holocene Accretionary Topography and Sea-Level Change* 1969. 156 pp.

123. WHITNEY, JOSEPH B. R. *China: Area, Administration and Nation Building* 1970. 198 pp.

124. EARICKSON, ROBERT. *The Spatial Behavior of Hospital Patients: A Behavioral Approach to Spatial Interaction in Metropolitan Chicago* 1970. 198 pp.

125. DAY, JOHN C. *Managing the Lower Rio Grande: An Experience in International River Development* 1970. 277 pp.

126. MAC IVER, IAN. *Urban Water Supply Alternatives: Perception and Choice in the Grand Basin Ontario* 1970. 178 pp.

127. GOHEEN, PETER G. *Victorian Toronto, 1850 to 1900: Pattern and Process of Growth* 1970. 278 pp.

128. GOOD, CHARLES M. *Rural Markets and Trade in East Africa* 1970. 252 pp.

129. MEYER, DAVID R. *Spatial Variation of Black Urban Households* 1970. 127 pp.

130. GLADFELTER, BRUCE. *Meseta and Campiña Landforms in Central Spain: A Geomorphology of the Alto Henares Basin.* 1971. 204 pp.

131. NEILS, ELAINE M. *Reservation to City: Indian Urbanization and Federal Relocation* 1971. 200 pp.

132. MOLINE, NORMAN T. *Mobility and the Small Town, 1900–1930* 1971. 169 pp.

133. SCHWIND, PAUL J. *Migration and Regional Development in the United States* 1971. 170 pp.

134. PYLE, GERALD F. *Heart Disease, Cancer and Stroke in Chicago: A Geographical Analysis with Facilities Plans for 1980.* 1971. 292 pp.

135. JOHNSON, JAMES F. *Renovated Waste Water: An Alternative Source of Municipal Water Supply in the U.S.* 1971. 155 pp.

136. BUTZER, KARL W. *Recent History of an Ethiopian Delta: The Omo River and the level of Lake Rudolf.* 1971. 184 pp.

137. HARRIS, CHAUNCY D. *Annotated World List of Selected Current Geographical Serials in English, French, and German* 3rd edition 1971. 77 pp.

138. HARRIS, CHAUNCY D., and FELLMANN, JEROME D. *International List of Geographical Serials* 2nd edition 1971. 267 pp.

139. MC MANIS, DOUGLAS R. *European Impressions of the New England Coast, 1497–1620* 1972. 147 pp.

140. COHEN, YEHOSHUA S. *Diffusion of an Innovation in an Urban System: The Spread of Planned Regional Shopping Centers in the United States, 1949–1968* 1972. 136 pp.